T0339659

Leadership Humility

This book deals in depth with an ancient attribute of effective leaders that has in recent years caught the attention of leadership writers and researchers. Today's effective leader is expected to demonstrate humility in addition to standard leadership attributes such as self-confidence, high-level cognitive skills, creativity, charisma, and the ability to articulate visions. The theme of this book is that leadership and professional effectiveness are enhanced when interspersed with other key leadership attributes including those mentioned above, assertiveness, a sense of humor, and strategic thinking ability. Many brash and aggressive successful leaders would be even more successful if they sprinkled their leadership approach with humility.

This book describes an opinion about the most relevant aspects of humility as it applies to leadership and professional effectiveness, yet the emphasis is on leadership. Equally important, each chapter contains suggestions for making better use of humility. Humility as it relates to leadership and professional effectiveness is covered from many angles. Among these topics are the many meanings and components of humility and how leadership humility impacts group member performance and behavior. We also describe the attributes of humble leaders and professionals and their type of interpersonal relationships. Servant leadership, because of its tie-in with humility, receives a separate chapter.

A description is provided about how narcissism, hubris, and charisma can be blended with humility to improve leadership effectiveness. Two other key topics are developing and enhancing your humility and making effective use of humility in leadership and professional life. The major contribution of this book is its systematic presentation of applied information about humility related to leadership effectiveness, such as the impact of humility on job performance and employee behavior, and how humility is part of servant leadership. At the same time, the book provides practical guidelines for applying the information to make optimum use of humility in the workplace.

Leadership Humility

A Characteristic that Enhances Professional Effectiveness

Andrew J. DuBrin

Routledge
Taylor & Francis Group
A PRODUCTIVITY PRESS BOOK

First published 2025

by Routledge
605 Third Avenue, New York, NY 10158

and by Routledge
4 Park Square, Milton Park, Abingdon, Oxon, OX14 4RN

Routledge is an imprint of the Taylor & Francis Group, an informa business

© 2025 Andrew J. DuBrin

The right of Andrew J. DuBrin to be identified as author of this work has been asserted by them in accordance with sections 77 and 78 of the Copyright, Designs and Patents Act 1988.

ISBN: 978-1-032-61056-6 (hbk)
ISBN: 978-1-032-61055-9 (pbk)
ISBN: 978-1-003-46178-4 (ebk)

DOI: 10.4324/9781003461784

Typeset in Minion
by Deanta Global Publishing Services, Chennai, India

Contents

Preface

Leadership Humility: A Characteristic that Enhances Professional Effectiveness deals in depth with an ancient attribute of effective leaders that has in recent years caught the attention of leadership writers and researchers. We include corporate professionals in our study because they as well as people in formal leadership positions influence and help others. Today's effective leader is expected to demonstrate humility in addition to standard leadership attributes such as self-confidence, high-level cognitive skills, creativity, charisma, and the ability to articulate visions.

Humility has many meanings, as will be described in Chapter 1, but as a starting point the following definition will point in the direction of the key topic of this book: Humility is a combination of self-awareness, appreciating the strengths and combinations of other, openness to ideas from others, and feedback regarding's one's performance. A leader or professional with humility is also by definition quite often humble.

The theme of this book is that leadership and professional effectiveness is enhanced when interspersed with other key leadership attributes including those mentioned above, assertiveness, a sense of humor, and strategic thinking ability. Many brash and aggressive successful leaders would be even more successful if they sprinkled their leadership approach with humility.

This book describes research and opinion about the most relevant aspects of humility as it applies to leadership and professional effectiveness, yet the emphasis is on leadership. Equally important, each chapter contains suggestions for making better use of humility. Some of the suggestions are provided in a box inserted at the end of each chapter, labeled *Guidelines for Action*. A self-quiz and/or checklist is provided in nine chapters to help the reader personalize the major idea under consideration. Among the self-quizzes are those related to humility, narcissism, servant leadership, and big-picture thinking. Most key points throughout the book are illustrated with examples including those of specific people. Nine of the chapters include a case history of a business leader who demonstrates humility including Mary Barra, CEO of General Motors.

Humility as it relates to leadership and professional effectiveness is covered from many angles. Among these topics are the many meanings and components of humility, and how leadership humility impacts group member performance and behavior We also describe the attributes of humble leaders and professionals, and their type of interpersonal relationships. Servant leadership, because of its tie-in with humility, receives a separate chapter. A description is provided about how narcissism, hubris, and charisma can be blended with humility to improve leadership effectiveness. Two other key topics are developing and enhancing your humility, and making effective use of humility in leadership and professional life.

Acknowledgments

Thanks go to the humble leaders and professionals I have known personally over the years who have provided me with insights into humility in the workplace. Leaders and professionals who are the antithesis of humility I have known personally and read about have also provided me useful insights for this book. Additional thanks go to the staff at Productivity Press who worked with me to publish *Leadership Humility*, my Publisher Michael Sinocchi, and my editorial assistant Samantha Dalton.

Finally, writing without loved ones would be a lonely task. My thanks therefore go to my family: Drew, Heidi, Douglas, Gizella, Melanie, Justin, Rosie, Clare, Michael, Camila, Sofia, Eliana, Julian, Carson, and Owen. Thank also to another part of my family, Stefanie, the woman in my life, and her daughter Sofia.

About the Author

Andrew J. DuBrin is Professor Emeritus of Management in the Saunders College of Business at the Rochester Institute of Technology, where he has taught courses and conducts research in management, organizational behavior, leadership, and human resource management. He has served the college as chairman of the management department and as team leader. He received his PhD in industrial psychology from Michigan State University, and an MS in Industrial Psychology at Purdue University. His business experience is in human resource management, and he consults with organizations and with individuals. His specialties include leadership and career management.

Professor DuBrin is an established author of trade titles, scholarly books, and textbooks. He also has written for professional journals and magazines. His trade titles cover many current issues, including leadership, coaching and mentoring, team play, office politics, coping with adversity, and big-picture thinking. His scholarly books include the subjects of crisis leadership, impression management, narcissism, and proactive personality. He has written textbooks on leadership, managerial psychology, business psychology, human resource management, introduction to management, political behavior in organizations, and human relations.

1

The Meaning and Components of Humility

During the last 30 years an ancient attribute of effective leaders has grabbed the attention of leadership writers and researchers. Today's effective leaders are expected to demonstrate humility and be humble in addition to standard leadership attributes such as self-confidence, high-level cognitive skills, charisma, and the ability to articulate visions. Although humility is expected of leaders, the same quality is expected of corporate professionals as well as those in independent practice. For example, most people who hire a financial planner welcome that person to not have all the answers but to be humble enough to listen carefully and understand their (the client's) perspective.

A starting point in understanding the meaning of humility is the most oft-repeated definition in articles about the subject. Humility is "not thinking less of yourself but thinking of yourself less." (This quote is attributed to C. S. Lewis, but a fact-check reveals that he is not the source.)[1] The humble leader or professional makes a deliberate effort to think about the needs and demands of the people he or she is leading. A *leader* is not only the person at the head of the organization, but anyone at any organizational level who attempts to influence others to attain important goals.

A humble leader or professional focuses on the needs of others without being self-centered. The humble leader recognizes that he or she does not have all the answers to problems facing the group. Instead, the leader listens carefully to the opinions and viewpoints of others before making a decision. A humble leader or professional may have creative ideas for moving the group or organization forward, but also welcomes the input of others.

DOI: 10.4324/9781003461784-1

The theme of this book is that humility is an important component of leadership and professional effectiveness that should be blended with other positive qualities. Several leadership experts have gone overboard with the assertion that humility is the one defining characteristic of leadership success. In reality, many other characteristics facilitate leadership success, such as assertiveness, creativity, self-confidence, and strategic thinking.

As a starting point in personalizing the study of humility for leadership and professional effectiveness, take the accompanying self-quiz. The answers in the direction of humility may appear obvious, but that is our intention. The purpose of this self-quiz as well as those presented in the other chapters is for you to engage in self-reflection, rather than to surprise you with the results of the quiz.

SELF-EVALUATION OF MY HUMILITY

Humble people, of course, find it difficult to perceive themselves as being humble. Nevertheless, taking this self-quiz will help sensitize you to aspects of your own behavior and attitudes that could reflect your level of humility. Because the results of this quiz are not being used for somebody else to judge your level of humility, there is no point in attempting to create a positive impression.

Statement Related to Humility	Mostly Agree	Mostly Disagree
1. Almost everybody who knows me well thinks that I have exceptional interpersonal skills.		
2. I carefully listen to other people without finishing their sentences for them.		
3. I enjoy listening to other people describe their accomplishments.		
4. When things go wrong, I look first to blame other people.		
5. It annoys me when other people give me advice on the job.		
6. I rarely applaud other people's accomplishments.		
7. I usually laugh louder than other people at my own jokes.		

Statement Related to Humility	Mostly Agree	Mostly Disagree
8. It annoys me when others on the job do not say positive things about my accomplishments.		
9. I have a strong desire to learn and improve.		
10. With few exceptions, I am the smartest person in the room.		
11. I get very upset whenever I am in conflict with other people.		
12. I am willing to admit my mistakes and limitations.		
13. I tend to ignore information that might require me to change my plans.		
14. I would lose respect if I admitted my limitations to others.		
15. I deserve a lot of respect from other people.		
16. I have much more talent than most of my co-workers.		
17. I have many more useful skills than most of my co-workers.		
18. I welcome feedback on my performance.		
19. I welcome feedback on my job-related behavior.		
20. I am willing to learn from others.		
21. I admit when I do not know how to do something,		
22. Unless another person is an established expert in his or field, I do not take that person's advice seriously.		
23. It is difficult for a person with talent like mine to be humble.		
24. I pay careful attention to the strengths of other people.		
25. I brag about myself a lot on social media.		

Scoring and Interpretation: Score yourself one point for each of the following questions you answered "*Mostly Agree*": 2, 3, 9, 12, 18, 19, 20, 21, and 24. Score yourself one point for each of the following questions you answered "*Mostly Disagree*": 1, 4, 5, 6, 7, 8, 10, 11, 13, 14, 15, 16, 16, 16, 17, 22, 23, and 25. If you scored 20 points or higher your self-evaluation suggests that you have an appropriate degree of humility to facilitate your leadership and professional effectiveness. If you scored between 6 and 19 points, you might need to practice more humility to facilitate your leadership and professional effectiveness. If you scored 5 or fewer points, you might be projecting an image of a person so humble and lacking in self-confidence that it detracts from your leadership and professional effectiveness.

Source: A few of the ideas for the statements in this quiz are based on the following sources: Arménio Rego, Miguel Pina E Cunha, and Ace Volkmann Simpson, "The Perceived Impact of Humility on Team Effectiveness: An Empirical Study," *Journal of Business Ethics*, March 2008, pp. 205–218; Bradley P. Owens, Michael D. Johnson, and Terence B. Mitchell, "Expressed Humility in Organizations," *Organization Science*, September–October 2013, pp. 1317–1338.

A VARIETY OF DEFINITIONS AND MEANINGS OF HUMILITY

A challenge in practicing humility or being humble is that the attribute is more complicated and nuanced than most people think. The simplest definition of humility is that it is the quality of being humble. And humble refers to being marked by meekness or modesty in behavior, attitude, or spirit—the opposite of being arrogant or prideful (*The American Heritage Dictionary*). Humility, as applied to leadership and professional behavior, is much more complicated. Carefully examining a variety of definitions of humility as it applies to the workplace will help clarify what being humble means in practice.

1. Humility is personal honesty that you do not know everything, and do not have the answer to every work-related problem. Humility enables you to question the flattery you receive, to admit your mistakes and weaknesses, and to be willing to listen to people who challenge your viewpoint.[2] The point about flattery is a good one

because the humble leader or professional recognizes that flattery is sometimes insincere and might be used as a method for the flatterer to gain advantage.

2. The word humility stems from the Latin word "humus" meaning "earth" or "ground," and also from the Latin word "humilis" referring to "on the ground." A humble person is therefore "down to earth" or "grounded." In common use, humility refers to having a grounded view of oneself. A grounded view of the self enables a humble person to acknowledge his or her personal qualities and limitations, without having feelings of superiority or inferiority.[3]

3. From a broad perspective, humility is defined as (a) self-awareness, (b) appreciating the strength and contributions of others, and (c) openness to ideas and feedback regarding one's performance. As a consequence of this meaning of humility, humble leaders have a better comprehension of organizational needs and make more informed decisions about the performance of tasks.[4]

4. The condition of humility is a down to earth, patient, compassionate, and concerned approach toward others. Humble leaders act with modesty and restraint and are interested in what others have to say. Humility also implies a person is willing to listen and change. A humble leader or professional makes an objective self-evaluation and recognizes personal limitations and mistakes. He or she also values the opinion of dissenters, and carefully weighs their criticisms.[5]

5. Leader humility is an interpersonal characteristic that facilitates leaders being able to cope better with social interactions by expressing a willingness to have an accurate self-perception, and to display appreciation of others and their ability to learn.[6] A humble leader would therefore work well with others by relying on personal strengths, but would also recognize when other members of the group have the more relevant expertise to deal with a work problem.

6. Humility is appropriate self-awareness that avoids thinking too highly of oneself, blended with a healthy self-respect that avoids thinking too lowly of oneself. This combination enables us to realistically assess our accomplishments while continuing to pursue personal and professional development.[7] Using this definition as a guide, the person who wants to be humble would attempt to attain a positive but realistic self-perspective.

7. Humility refers to understanding your strengths and weaknesses, while at the same time recognizing the strengths of others.[8] Although this definition simplifies humility, it does focus on two key elements of humility: self-awareness and a focus on the contributions of group members.

8. A scientific definition of humility states: "Although humility frequently is equated with a sense of unworthiness and low self-regard, theoreticians view true humility as a rich, multifaced construct that entails an accurate assessment of one's characteristics, and ability to acknowledge limitations, and a 'forgetting of the self.'"[9] Again, humility is viewed as including an accurate self-assessment while at the same time thinking more about other people than the self.

9. Humility is a stable and enduring trait reflecting a person's sense that he or she is not the center of the universe.[10] A contribution of this definition is that points to the idea that a humble leader or professional downplays arrogance, hubris, and narcissism. Instead, he or she recognizes the importance of his or her constituents.

10. Prominent humility researcher Bradley Owens explains that at the root of humble leadership is self-transcendence. Humble leaders temper or tame the ego and embrace a leadership perspective that seeks to elevate everyone.[11] Transcendence also refers to looking beyond the self to help others and recognize a broader purpose of the organization or organizational unit. The implications of this definition are profound. The humble leader or professional does not forget about the self, yet still seeks ways to improve the lives of other people.

Definition number 3 is particularly useful in pointing you toward how humility contributes to leadership and professional effectiveness. *Humility in this sense is a combination of self-awareness, appreciating the strengths and contributions of others, and openness to ideas and feedback regarding one's performance.* As the term humility is used throughout this book, this definition fits the best.

The Components and Dimensions of Humility

The components or elements of humility relate closely to its dimensions but provide more insight into what humility means in practice. Studying the many components of humility will provide you with some useful ideas for being a humble leader or professional.

Nine Components Based on Interviews with Managers

Interviews were conducted with a total of 332 managers in Singapore to explore the components of leader humility. Conducting a study in Singapore was particularly useful because humility is embedded in many Asian cultures. Nine dimensions were identified that provide an in-depth explanation of what leader humility entails.[12] Other studies that have investigated leader humility usually identify several of these dimensions. The nine dimensions follow, including statements of the particular dimension in practice.

1. *Having an accurate view of self.* (Good self-awareness about own strengths and weaknesses and acknowledging personal flaws.)
2. *Recognition of strengths and achievements of group members.* (A humble leader acknowledges contributions from followers when he or she succeeds.)
3. *Acts as a model of willingness to learn, and ability to correct behavior.* (Accepts feedback on his or her performance from subordinates and is willing to listen and learn from them.) In another study Professors Bradley Owens and David Hackman asked 16 CEOs, 20 mid-level leaders, and 19 front-line leaders to describe specifically how humble workplace leaders operate, and how they differ from non-humble leaders. Although the leaders were from different types of organizations—military, manufacturing, healthcare, retailing, and religious—they agreed on one key point: The essence of leader humility involves being a model to group members of how to grow personally.[13]
4. *Leading by example.* (The humble leader is willing to do the things that he or she asks followers to do, such as preparing PowerPoint slides.)
5. *Displaying modesty.* (Willing to let other people be in the spotlight and keeps a low profile even when successful.) Displaying modesty has also been framed as having a low self-focus. Humility therefore also involves a forgetting about the self in order to focus on group organizational problems, and the best interest of other people.[14] For

example, a chief marketing officer recognizes that she is an internal candidate for the CEO position. Although this potential dramatic shift in her career is on her mind, because she has a low self-focus, she blocks thoughts about the promotion from interfering with her leadership and management responsibilities.

6. *Working together for the collective good.* (Able to work together with the staff to attain a common good, including staying late to complete a project.)

7. *Empathy and approachability.* (Leads with high emotional intelligence, including being kind and caring toward group members.)

8. *Showing mutual respect and fairness.* (A humble leader treats group members impartially.)

9. *Mentoring and coaching.* (A humble leader is willing to coach employees on their personal development.)

In the remaining discussion of the dimensions of humility, we will not repeat these dimensions even though they have been identified in other studies.

Valuing Others

This component of humility refers to the capacity to see others not only in terms of what they can do at present but in terms of their highest potential. With this perception the leader is able to forge relationships that complement their own skill sets with those of others. Valuing the worth of others facilitates making connections between the parties.

Valuing others also enables the leader to empower group members because he or she is convinced of their potential contribution. When you value others, their skills and abilities are appreciated and considered important.[15]

Constant Learning

Self-awareness inspires the leader or professional to constantly improve, to acquire more advanced skills, and to acquire knowledge in a quest for a better life. The motivation to learn is focused on using the new knowledge to create a better world. The ability to constantly learn requires an understanding of a constantly changing world. Also required is a recognition of the importance of using wisdom and knowledge for self-improvement and the improvement of others. The constant learner also sees the need to utilize information effectively. As with the other dimensions or components of humility, the leader or professional may not find it easy to squeeze in the time to be a constant learner. Yet a few minutes of reflection here and there can enable one to acquire some new useful knowledge. An example would be reading. An article about how autistic people make good coders, and seeing what the company might do to capitalize on this insight.

Openness

Being open refers to encouraging dissent and valuing truth over coverups. A leader with openness is willing to ask for and implement the suggestions of others, including advice about how he or she could do a better job as a manager, leader, or professional.[16]

Awareness of Relationships with Others. As a consequence of several of the other components or dimensions of humility, humble leaders or professionals are keenly aware of their interpersonal relationships, and express empathy and respect for others. These leaders and professionals know that they are part of a community instead of being absorbed with the self. The awareness of relationships with others provides a leadership advantage because emotions are taken into account in dealing with people.[17] For example, an IT professional might reflect, "I am trying to help this person deal with ransomware, but until I help him overcome his sense of panic it will be difficult to help."

An example of a humble leader is Katrina Lake, the founder and CEO of Stitch Fix, the clothing and accessories subscription service. The company uses algorithms and expert stylists to select (or "curate") a box of clothing for clients. Lake is a likable, stylish, and energetic person, who built the company up to over $1 billion in annual sales, combining data analytics with a human touch. Lake can readily be classified as a charismatic and transformational leader, yet at the same time, she shows humility in dealing with employees and customers. She listens to and understands customers and takes a personal interest in many employees. Although the CEO, Lake takes time to help clients individually. Her humility and charisma are reflected in the devotion she engenders in employees, and the many people wanting to work with and for her.[18]

Despite Lake's fine leadership qualities including humility, Stitch Fix continues to struggle financially, suggesting that leadership humility does not always guarantee financial success.

HUMILITY AS A VIRTUE

A perspective about humility and leadership with ancient roots is that humility is a virtue because religious leaders were supposed to be humble. Given that humility usually includes recognizing and appreciating knowledge and guidance outside of oneself, it is a basic principle of the major religions. Philosophers have identified humility as a "meta-virtue" that is a foundation for other virtues including forgiveness, courage, wisdom, and compassion.

Humility is also said to undergird other virtues such as forgiveness, courage, and wisdom because humility is a "temperance virtue" meaning that it constrains excess. The person who is virtuous will follow a "golden mean" and avoid excesses such as giving so much money to charity that his or her own family suffers. In short, when humility is regarded as a virtue, it fits the historical idea of being a classical source of strength that moves a person toward a realistic self-perspective.

The ancient Greeks looked upon humility as a virtuous trait, but it was not heavily emphasized. To the Greek philosophers, humility was not based on lack of arrogance, but on the understanding of human limitations. (A humble leader would therefore not place unrealistic demands on subordinates.) An educated person was thought to readily understand the importance of humility.

In the modern era, humility has been identified as a core organizational virtue proposed to provide the foundation for moral action in the workplace. Furthermore, humility is thought to encourage positive behaviors that exceed the norm such as exceptional job performance and motivation to help co-workers. Virtues such as humility have been viewed by scholars as those that are good, humanitarian, and facilitate human betterment.[19] What is "good, humanitarian, and facilitates human betterment" is, of course, a subjective judgment. A person making the judgment might decide that the CEO of a gun manufacturer is not "good," yet the leader in question is providing an opportunity for company employees and suppliers to earn a living. The CEO is also adding to the life satisfaction of hunters.

FOUR TYPES OF HUMILITY

An advanced understanding of how humility contributes to leadership and professional effectiveness includes the idea that humility exists in different forms or types. As a basic example, supervisor Carlos might be humble about his athletic ability but not his intellect. The various types of humility contribute to leadership and professional effectiveness. One basic type of humility is the type we feel around elders and dignitaries. For people who incorporate the value that authority should be respected, this is a natural type of humility. Department head Kaitlin might feel and act superior to subordinates but she becomes humble and deferent when in the presence of the 75-year-old company founder.

A second basic type of humility is the humility we feel in the presence of people who put us in awe of their achievements. Team leader Jason might not ordinarily be humble but when his team receives a visit from the scientists whose inventions were the foundation of the company, Jason feels a sense of humility.

A third basic type of humility is the here-and-now humility a person experiences when dependent on another person. Renowned organizational psychologist Edgar Schein explains that here-and-now humility is how you feel when dependent on another person. You feel, "My status is inferior to yours at this moment because you know something or can do something that I need to accomplish my task or goal. I have to be humble because I am temporarily dependent on you."[20] This is the type of humility many of us experience when we have a software failure such as not being able to access the internet. The humility in this moment of frustration and dread is expressed toward the tech support person who applies his or her skill and knowledge to regain our internet access.

A fourth type of humility deals heavily with our thinking patterns. According to research conducted at Duke University, *intellectual humility* is a type of humility that may influence people's decision-making abilities in politics, health, and other arenas. Intellectual humility is an awareness that one's beliefs may be wrong. Researchers led by social psychologist Mark Leary found no difference between liberals and conservatives or between religious and nonreligious people with respect to intellectual humility.[21]

An everyday expression suggesting intellectual humility is "I could be wrong." Brittany, the head of a real-estate agency, believed strongly that single males without a live-in partner would only be interested in purchasing a condominium, not a detached house. Soon two agents in her office sold detached houses to single middle-aged males. Showing intellectual humility, Brittany told her agents, "Thanks gang. My stereotype about single males only wanting to purchase a condominium home has been smashed. It's nice to learn something new about the real-estate business."

Intellectual humility is the polar opposite of intellectual arrogance or conceit. This type of humility resembles open-mindedness. Intellectually humble people might have strong beliefs, but they recognize their fallibility. As with Brittany, they are willing to be proven wrong on matters large and small.

According to Leary, intellectual humility has potential benefits in the workplace. He says, "If you're sitting around a table at a meeting, and the boss is very low in intellectual humility, he or she isn't going to listen to other people's suggestions." The problem with low intellectual humility by the person in charge of the meeting is that good leadership requires taking into account many perspectives.

A key lesson from the research on intellectual humility is that not being afraid of being wrong is a useful value. Leary says that if everyone was a bit more intellectually humble, they would get along better and be less frustrated with each other.

WHAT HUMILITY IS NOT

A deep understanding of what humility is not will help propel a person toward an effective use of humility for influencing others. The traditional definition of humility is the worst offender for purposes of being humble to enhance leadership and professional effectiveness. According to a negatively toned definition, humility is a sign of perceiving oneself to have little self-worth. This definition has led to a pervasive misconception that humility is a weakness, reflecting the core belief, "I am not worth it."[22] Having very low self-esteem, a person is likely to make frequent statements such as, "I'm not an expert," "I'm only a lay person," "I'm not sure," or "It's just my opinion." In contrast, people with effective humility have high self-worth and self-esteem. They listen carefully to the opinions and viewpoints of subordinates, customers, and clients but recognize that they have an important role to play in guiding others.

Having high self-esteem, the leader or professional with humility is self-aware with a reasonably good estimate of the self. For example, a humble brand manager at a consumer-goods company might think,

> *I know I am pretty good at brand promotion, but there are two people in the group who are much stronger at product design. I'll get in touch with Zoe and Gerry to help come up with a good package design for our new product.*

A similar line of reasoning about what humility is not, is that being humble in the workplace is not self-abasement or a lack of self-confidence. When we see ourselves as less worthy than other people, we are just as self-focused as when being arrogant. With a mindset of feeling less worthy than others, it is difficult to be as aware of or helpful to others as true humility requires. For example, a person who feels less worthy than others might fear that his or her imperfections would be observed and judged. As a result, the person focuses on projecting a positive image as perceived by others.[23] Finance specialist Amanda Thomas observes similarly that humility is not self-depreciation or ripping on yourself. Such behavior sets a bad example for future leaders who think they must put themselves down while interacting with others in to gain their respect.[24]

Another helpful perspective is that being a humble leader or professional also does not mean being subservient. Executive business coach Paulette Ashlin says that a humble leader needs to be assertive while depending on other people. An effective humble leader collaborates with others. Humble leaders who get into trouble are those who are subservient and do whatever others ask them to do. True humility is not simply pleasing other people but holding oneself and the group accountable for results.[25]

A common mistake is to associate humility with false modesty.[26] A person with effective humility accepts praise and compliments yet can still share the praise with contributors to the effort. Assume that team leader Duff is told by a manager that he has done an outstanding job this last quarter. Ineffective humility would be to say, "I really didn't do anything. It was the team that produced the good results." A more positive form of humility would be to respond, "I appreciate the compliment. I am proud of what the team and I accomplished this previous quarter."

GUIDELINES FOR ACTION

1. Finding an optimum level of humility for yourself could be a boost to your career. Being appropriately humble is an important contributor to leadership and professional effectiveness. We emphasize *appropriately* because many very humble people do not meet with much career success.

2. A useful starting point in refining your humility is to ask subordinates, co-workers, clients, or customers their opinion on how to resolve a problem. Welcoming input from others is a key indicator of humility. Welcoming input is also a subtle way of recognizing the strengths of others.

3. A supreme act of humility is to improve the lives of other people. Improving the lives of others could take many forms including coaching others, recommending them for promotion, and giving them realistic compliments to boost their self-confidence.

4. Humility requires self-awareness, meaning that you have to develop a realistic understanding of your strengths and weaknesses. Listening carefully to feedback about yourself including compliments and negative comments facilitates developing self-awareness.

5. A potent way of projecting humility is to show empathy and respect for others. Many successful leaders carefully listen to another person's point of view and are respectful of workers at all job levels, suggesting the humility of these leaders.

6. Working on developing intellectual humility because not only is it effective in leading others it projects an excellent human quality. A guide to being intellectually humble is to recognize that your

viewpoint has merit, but you are willing to give other opinions a fair chance.

7. A key starting point in using humility to your advantage in leadership and professional roles is to shake the traditional definition of humility as perceiving oneself to have little self-worth. Even if this definition is correct in some circumstances, it detracts from the positive aspects of humility. A particularly useful definition of humility is that it combines self-awareness, appreciation of the strengths and contributions of others, and openness to ideas and feedback regarding one's performance.

NOTES

1. Trevor Schakohl, www.checkyourfact.com, June 30, 2019, p. 1.
2. David Shedd, "Humility, A Leadership Attribute Throughout the Ages," www.businessinsider.com, April 1, 2011, p. 1.
3. Bradley P. Owens, Wade C. Rowatt, and Alan L Wilkins, "Exploring the Relevance and Implications of Humility in Organizations." In Kim Cameron and Gretchen Spreitzer (Eds.), *Handbook of Positive Organizational Scholarship* (New York: Oxford University Press, 2011).
4. Robert Hogan as cited in Neal Burgis, "Importance of Humility in Your Leadership," www.successful-solutions.com, February 29, 2019, p. 1.
5. Pareena G. Lawrence, "Neohumility/Humility and Business Leadership: Do They Belong Together?" *Journal of Business and Leadership*, No. 1, 2008, pp. 116–126.
6. Wenxing Liu, Jianghua Mao, and Xiao Chen, "Leader Humility and Team Innovation: Investigating the Substituting Role of Task Interdependence and the Mediating Role of Team Voice Climate," *Frontiers in Psychology*, June 30, 2017, p. 4.
7. Erik Hoestra, Anthony Bell, and Scott R. Peterson, "Humility in Leadership: Abandoning the Pursuit of Unattainable Behavior." In S. A. Quatro & R. R. Sims (Eds.), *Executive Ethics: Ethical Dilemmas and Challenges for the C-Suite* (Greenwich, CT: Information Age Publishing, 2008), p. 7.
8. Karin Fabian, *Business News Daily*, March 6, 2017, p. 1.
9. June Price Tangney, "Humility: Theoretical Perspectives, 'Empirical Findings and Directions for Future Research,'" *Journal of Social and Clinical Psychology* No. 1, p. 70.
10. Christopher Peterson and Martin Seligman, *Character Strengths and Virtues: A Handbook of Classification* (New York: Oxford University Press, 2004).
11. Quoted in Jamie Aten, "How Humble Leaders Foster Resilience," *Psychology Today* (www.psychologytoday.com), February 26, 2019, p. 1.
12. Oc Burak et al. *Leader Humility in Singapore, The Leadership Quarterly*, February 2015, pp. 68–80.
13. Bradley P. Owens and David R. Hekman, "Modeling How to Grow: An Inductive Examination of Humble Leader Behaviors, Contingencies, and Outcomes," *Academy of Management Journal*, August 2012, pp. 787–818.

14. Bradley P. Owens, "Humility in Organizational Leadership," Doctoral Dissertation University of Washington, 2009, p. 13.
15. This and the following dimension are from C. Caldwell, "Love and Humility— Enhancing Leadership Success," *JResLit Journal of Business Administration & Management*, Issue 1, 2019, p. 2.
16. Lawrence, "Neohumility/Humility and Business Leadership," pp. 12–13.
17. "Servant Leadership: Humility," RitzCarltonleadershipcenter.com, July 20, 2016, pp. 1–3.
18. Connie Loizos, "Katrina Lake is Back as Interim CEO of Struggling Stitch Fix, 17 Months after Stepping Down," *TC* (www.techcrinch.com), January 25, 2023, pp. 1–5; Sara Spellings, "How I Get It Done: Stitch Fix CEO Katrina Lake," *The Cut* (the-cut.com), December 30, 2019, pp. 1–2; "The World's Most Innovative Companies: Stitch Fix: For Sizing Ups Its Customers," *Fast Company*, March/April 2018, p. 44.
19. The preceding three paragraphs are based on Owens and Hekman, "Modeling How to Grow: An Inductive Examination of Humble Leader Behaviors, Contingencies, and Outcomes," p. 788, and Richard Martin, "Humility as a Desirable personality Trait and a Construct of Effective Leadership: A Review of the Literature," unpublished manuscript, Regent University, 2014, p. 6.
20. The three types of humility, but not the explanation and examples are from Edgar H. Schein and Peter A. Schein, *Humble Leadership: The Power of Relationships, Openness and Trust* (Oakland, CA: Berrett-Kohler, 2018).
21. Mark R. Leary et al, "Cognitive and Interpersonal Features of Intellectual Humility," *Personality and Social Psychology Bulletin*, March 17, 2017. DOI: 10.1177/0146167217697695. pp. 1–16; Alison Jones, "For a Modest Personality Trait 'Intellectual; Humility' Packs a Punch," *Research*, March 11, 2017, pp. 1–3.
22. Marie-Michèle Beauchesne, "CEO Humility: Development of an Unobtrusive Measure and Strategic Implications," *FIU Electronic Theses and Dissertations*, 2014. 1617, p. 4.
23. "What Humility is Not," *The Arbinger Institute* (www.arbingerinstitute.com), November 1, 2017, pp. 1–3.
24. Amanda Thomas, "Set a Leadership Example through Humility," www.cuinsight.com, December 29, 2017, p. 2.
25. "Leaders as Learners: Humility is at the Heart of Great Leadership," (Interview with Paulette Ashlin), www.globalgirldproject.org, October 28, 2014, p. 2.
26. Martin Luendink, "The Virtue of Humility," www.cleverism.com, September 17, 2016, p. 2.

2

The Performance Impact of Humility

A major justification for investing time into studying humility for leaders and professionals in the workplace is that such behavior has an impact on performance. The performance, or results, could be at the individual, group, or organizational level. Humility might be an admirable virtue, but it warrants more attention when we look at its performance consequences.

Humility as it relates to its impact on other people has been referred to as *expressed humility*. In other words, the humble leader says things or does things that suggest humility. A prime example is the humble leader saying to a subordinate, "How do you think we should proceed?" To help you focus on expressed humility, take the accompanying quiz that gives you the opportunity to evaluate the actions and attitudes of any leader or professional you have worked with.

EXPRESSED HUMILITY QUIZ

Here is an opportunity to evaluate the humility of a leader or professional you know now or from the past. In reference to the leader or professional you are describing, indicate your strength of agreement with each of the following statements: SD—*Strongly disagree*; D—*Disagree*; N—*Neutral*, A—*Agree*; SA—*Strongly agree*.

Statement about Humility	SD	D	N	A	SA
1. Asks the group a lot of questions before making a big decision.	1	2	3	4	5
2. Asks for feedback even if most likely would be critical.	1	3	3	4	5

DOI: 10.4324/9781003461784-2

Statement about Humility	SD	D	N	A	SA
3. Reminds the group occasionally that he or she has much more power than they do.	5	4	3	2	1
4. Has a great big, fat ego,	5	4	3	2	1
5. Admits when he or she does not know how to do something.	1	2	3	4	5
6. Relies on the skills and technical advice of group members.	1	2	3	4	5
7. Compliments other people on their strengths.	1	2	3	4	5
8. Shows appreciation for the contribution of others.	1	2	3	4	5
9. Will often make a statement similar to "You know more about this than I do."	1	2	3	4	5
10. Makes frequent reference to his or her career success.	5	4	3	2	1
11. Willing to learn from others.	1	2	3	4	5
12. Accomplishes a lot without asking for credit.	1	2	3	4	5
13. Talks about twice as much as anybody else in a face-to-face or virtual meeting.	5	4	3	2	1
14. Often thanks group members for their contribution.	1	2	3	4	5
15. I have heard him or her described as a "big jerk" on at least several occasions.	5	4	3	2	1

SCORING AND INTERPRETATION:

65–75: The person you describe is a highly humble leader or professional but runs the risk of not appearing self-confident and assertive.

40–74: The person you describe most likely has the right amount of humility to enhance his or her leadership and professional effectiveness.

15–39: The person you describe might be self-centered and narcissistic to the point that it detracts from his or he leadership and professional effectiveness.

Note: The idea for this quiz and several of the statements are based on Bradley P. Owens, Michael D. Johnson, and Terence R. Mitchell, "Expressed Humility in Organizations: Implications for Performance. Teams, and Leadership," *Organization Science*, September–October 2013, p. 1523.

LEADER HUMILITY AND INDIVIDUAL
JOB PERFORMANCE

Humility on the part of leaders and professionals can directly and indirectly influence the job performance of subordinates and clients in various ways. In this section we examine this idea from several standpoints, all supporting the idea that humility makes a positive difference in performance. We also look at a surprising finding about how humility can lower the need for the leader to be highly intelligent.

Humility of Professional Workers and Job Performance

A basic tenet of this book is that humility enhances the job performance of leaders and professionals. A field study demonstrated this relationship. Two researchers from Baylor University along with a business consultant surveyed 269 employees in 25 different companies across 20 different states. The employees were Direct Support Professionals who provided regular assisted living support to customers who needed medical care. The customers were described by the supervisors to be "mobile, verbal, with challenging behaviors." Among the challenges were refusal to comply with treatment, self-injurious behavior, and property destruction.

Supervisors of the Direct Support Professionals rated the job performance of each employee on 35 different job skills, and also described the kind of client with whom the employee worked. Three representative skills were (a) directly assisting in activities of daily living, (b) performing household chores, and (c) exhibiting compassion/tolerance. The ratings informed management of how the employees were performing, and enabled the researchers to examine which personality traits were linked to job performance ratings.

A major finding was that workers who scored higher on the traits of honesty and humility were rated significantly higher by their supervisors with respect to job performance. The researchers defined honesty and humility as exhibiting high levels of fairness, greed-avoidance, sincerity, and modesty.

The lead researcher, Wade Rowatt, a professor of psychology and neuroscience, said, "This study shows that those who possess the combination of honesty and humility have better job performance."

Furthermore, honesty–humility was more strongly associated with job performance than basic personality traits such as agreeableness and conscientiousness.[1]

Enhancing the Creativity of Group Members

Leaders who express humility often enhance the creativity of group members because they set up a climate conducive to imaginative thinking. The key idea is that a humble leader will often create a *psychologically safe* environment, meaning that staff members feel safe to take the risk of making a mistake. The person who feels psychologically safe believes he or she will not be punished or humiliated for speaking up about ideas, questions, concerns, or mistakes. Being creative involves just such behaviors.

A study demonstrating that humble leadership leads to psychological safety, and then to creativity, was conducted in the Guangdong province of China. Data was collected from employees and their immediate leaders in 50 software firms. The several departments targeted for research required substantial creativity, such as software research, new product development, and quality control. Team members rated their leader's humble leadership (similar to the quiz earlier in this chapter), and leaders rated employee creativity. Measures were also taken for psychological safety and how well team members shared knowledge with each other. The final sample was substantial, consisting of 106 team leaders and 328 team members.

The results of the study were complicated but shed light on the important relationship between leader humility and employee creativity. As mentioned at the outset, the major finding of the study was that humble leadership is positively related to psychological safety. In turn, psychological safety is positively related to employee creativity. Humble leadership therefore has an indirect influence on follower creativity via psychological safety.

Another indirect relationship the study demonstrated sheds additional light on the utility of humble leadership. Psychological safety appears to enhance employee creativity only when knowledge sharing exists in the group. The reason is that creativity is enhanced when members share ideas with each other is because combining ideas that were not previously combined is a big part of creativity. Leadership humility enters the picture because by being humble, and not knowing all the answers, the leader makes sharing knowledge worthwhile.[2] A team member might think, "It's useful to share my knowledge with others because we know that our good ideas might be put to use. Our team leader welcomes our input."

Humility Can Foster Employee Engagement

A study conducted by Bradley P. Owens and his co-researchers provided some evidence that leadership humility leads indirectly to employee engagement. Engagement is positively related to performance because a worker who is committed to the job and the company will invest extra effort to perform well. The study in question took place in a large US mid-western health organization, with 704 employees rating 218 leaders. A sample item from the job engagement scale was "I am immersed in my work." A key finding of the study was that leaders expressed humility was positively related to job engagement.

Digging further into the findings, the researchers suggested that a leader with humility helps establish a group climate in which people have the opportunity to learn and develop. A climate of this nature enables group members to invest more of themselves in their jobs. For many employees, the opportunity to learn is a job feature that makes them more excited about their work.[3]

Humility Can Lower the Need for the Very High Intelligence

A pioneering study on the impact of humility on job performance arrived at a finding that seemed surprising at the time. The study found that humble people with lower general mental ability may still perform well. One reason offered by the researchers is that a humble person might be more willing to learn the behaviors necessary to master the performance tasks.[4] Another explanation is equally plausible. Humble leaders usually recognize when they lack the expertise to solve a given problem and will therefore ask for help from the right people. Assume that Mark, a wealth manager, receives a request from a client to invest in a complex type of security that he does not understand well. Instead of bluffing, Mark asks another staff member for help in understanding the security. Mark now performs better as a wealth manager because he was humble enough to seek the expertise he needed to satisfy the client.

Leader Humility and Team Performance

Leadership humility often has a big impact on team performance. The humble leader seeks the cooperation of all team members, shows openness toward their ideas, and encourages them to become actively involved in solving problems the team is tackling.[5] In addition to this opinion, there is some quantitative research evidence about the impact of leader humility on team performance and effectiveness.

Owen and Heckman conducted a study with 84 laboratory teams and 77 organizational teams to see how leader humility impacted team performance. It was observed that when a leader admits to mistakes and takes action for the greater good, it creates an atmosphere of promoting group goals. Instead of internal competition, the team focuses on achieving its highest potential. The collective promotion of group goals becomes the foundation for better performance. By focusing on collective performance, group members tend to prioritize group performance and goals.

The study found that another benefit of an atmosphere of humility within the team is that employees are more comfortable sharing and generating ideas. (Psychological safety is beneficial again.) A few behaviors reflecting collective (or team) humility are as follows:

- The team falls short of reaching a performance goal, and members identify their areas of weakness, and how they can do a better job of contributing to group goals the next time.
- A new team member suggests an idea and the team implements the suggestion.
- One team member receives an award during a meeting and proceeds to identify the contribution of each team member to the accomplishment that merited the award.
- Team members feel they can voice opinions about teammates as well as accept constructive criticism.

The interpretation of the results of the study is that leader humility indirectly enhances team performance by fostering humble teams. In turn, the humble teams transcend competition with each other to perform better collectively. When leaders behave humbly, team members emulate their humble behaviors, leading to collective humility. The underlying mechanism is *social contagion* in which certain behaviors are followed by group members without much conscious thought.[6] You have most likely observed how smiles and politeness can be contagious within a group.

Another empirical study also supported the idea that team leader humility enhances team effectiveness indirectly. In this research, 96 leaders were studied, along with 307 subordinates, their 96 supervisors, and 656 peers of the leaders. Self-report measures of humility (such as the quiz in Chapter 1) were gathered along measures of observations by others (such as the quiz in this chapter.). The study found that leadership humility is indirectly related to how the leaders are perceived to have an impact on team effectiveness. The indirect factor here is that a humble leader encourages the balanced processing of information. In turn, the balanced processing results in the group members perceiving the leader as someone who contributes to team effectiveness.[7]

The takeaway from the two studies just reviewed is that even if the link between leadership humility and team performance is indirect, it is still beneficial. An analogy is that physical exercise itself does not make you a better problem solver, but it does increase blood flow to the brain that facilitates creative problem-solving.

LEADER HUMILITY AND ORGANIZATIONAL PERFORMANCE

A major justification for high-level leaders incorporating humility into their leadership style is that an appropriate dose of humble leadership will improve organizational performance. An example of this is Tim Cook, the CEO of Apple Inc., who shows many characteristics of a humble leader. He is open to contrary opinions, freely acknowledges the contributions of others, and is modest in his pronouncements. Apple may have been successful under the leadership of Steve Jobs, but the company has soared to new heights of sales volume, profitability, and market capitalization under the tenure of Cook. In this section we look at some reasonably strong evidence that humility at the top can improve organizational performance.

Leadership Humility in the Computer Software and Hardware Industry

Three management professors, Amy Y. Ou, David A. Waldman, and Suzanne Peterson, sought to explore if humble CEO leadership really helped a firm perform well. An impressive part of the study was the breadth of the organizations studied. The sample consisted of 105 firms in the computer software and hardware business in the United States. Ninety-two percent of the firms were privately held, and most were small-to-medium enterprises with sales of less than $5 million, and no more than 500 employees.

The sample was part of a broader data collection effort that examined executive leadership and firm performance over a period of several years. The CEOs and chief financial officers (CFOs) of the firms were surveyed twice during a series of executive consortiums. The consortiums were established to enable senior executives to network, share information, and learn from speakers and panelists.

CFOs were asked to complete a survey designed to evaluate their CEO's humility, and also charismatic leadership style. Also in this study, the humility measure was quite similar to the one presented earlier in this chapter. (Charisma was measured as a check on whether the results of the study could be attributed to charisma rather than humility.) Both the CEOs and CFOs categories of executives were also asked to rate how well the top-management teams were integrated. A sample item measuring integration was "When a team member is busy, other team members often volunteer to help manage the workload." Return on assets (ROA) was used as the measure of firm performance. Several other measures of how the leaders managed were taken and will be mentioned next in the results of the study.

The study found that CEO humility has implications for firm strategy and performance. Humble CEOs were found to build integrative top-management teams and promote pay equity among their top-management teams. (Integration in the top-management teams referred to more collaboration, sharing information, and possessing a shared vision.) The same CEOs established ambidextrous and profitable firms. (Organizational ambidexterity refers to an organization's ability to simultaneously take advantage of existing market opportunities and innovate to meet the challenges of future markets.) The researchers concluded that CEO humility has important implications for firm processes and outcomes. Collaboration is an example of a process, and an example of an outcome is a return on assets.[8]

Leadership Humility and Its Positive Impact on Top and Middle Managers

In addition to having a positive impact on the top-management team, CEO humility can also create an atmosphere for middle managers that leads to better outcomes for the organization. Amy Y. Ou and another set of colleagues conducted a study building on the results described in the previous section. The intent of this study was to develop additional insights into how CEO humility links to the actions and beliefs of both top and middle managers. Survey data were gathered twice from 328 top-management team members and 645 middle managers in 63 private companies in China, representing several industries. Qualitative data from interviews with 51 CEOs provided additional insight into how humility might impact an organization.[9]

Part of the reasoning behind the study in question was that unconstrained exercise of power and excessive self-importance can have damaging consequences for organizations. Humility, in contrast, recognizes that there is a purpose out there of more importance than the self, and that self-focus should be low. In the study in question found a measurable trickle-down effect of humility.

- CEO humility has a positive association with empowering members of the top-management team.
- Humble CEOs connect to top-level and middle-level managers via the collective perception that they are empowered.
- As a result of the empowering behaviors, the top-management team becomes more integrated.
- When the top-management team is integrated, middle managers perceive the organizational climate to be empowering.
- An empowering organizational climate is positively associated with the work engagement of middle managers, higher commitment, and job performance.

The researchers concluded that humble CEOs bring a broader perception of service to organizations that can inspire workers. Part of the inspiration stems from workers observing that their strengths are appreciated. The researchers also showed that CEO humility gains acceptance. For top-level and middle-level managers by appealing to collective interests and downplaying egotism.

Leadership Humility and Passion in Highly Successful Companies

The current interest in how leadership humility enhances organizational performance was stimulated by the research and writings of management consultant Jim Collins about how organizations go from good to great.[10] According to Collins, executives who blend the traits of personal humility with intense professionalism will are catalysts in transforming an organization from ordinary to extraordinary. His research showed that the essential ingredient for bringing a company to greatness is having a Level 5 leader—an executive who blends extreme personal humility with intense personal will or passion for organizational success. The characteristics common to Level 5 leaders are humility, will, ferocious resolve, and giving credit to others while assigning blame to themselves.

Out of the 1,435 Fortune 500 companies that Collins studied, only 11 achieved and sustained greatness, as measured by stock returns at least three times the average for 15 years after a major transition period. Stock market price, of course, is but one measure of the performance of a firm. Other valid include profitability, market share, product or service quality, and wages paid to employees. The study was conducted two decades ago, and two of these great companies were Gillette and Kimberly-Clark. The 11 companies with exceptional stock returns each had a Level 5 leader, who blended the paradoxical combination of deep personal humility with intense professional will.

How Collins and His Team Conducted Their Research

Discovering Level 5 leadership stemmed from a research project begun in 1996. Collins and his research teams were looking to answer one question: "Can a good company become a great company, and if the answer is Yes, how?" Many great companies had strong founders, such as George Merck and Walt Disney who instilled greatness in the early days of the company. The key issue for Collins was understanding how the vast majority of companies recognize at some point they are good but not great might elevate their status.

To understand this issue, the research teams looked for companies that had shifted from good performance to great performance and were able to sustain greatness. The researchers also identified companies that had failed to make that sustained shift. A study was conducted of the contrast between companies that can make and sustain a shift to greatness versus those that could have yet failed to do so.

A search was conducted for the specific pattern of cumulative stock returns at or below the general stock market level for 15 years, followed by a transition point, the cumulative returns of at least three times the stock market level over the next 15 years. The shift had to be distinct from the entire industry, otherwise the company was dropped from the study. Beginning with 1,435 companies that appeared on the Fortune 500 from 1965 to 1995, 15 good-to-great examples were identified.

With 22 research associates, the study involved a wide range of both qualitative and quantitative analyses. The qualitative aspect of the study involved scanning nearly 6,000 articles, 87 interviews with key executives, analyzing internal strategy documents, and culling through the reports of financial analysts. The quantitative aspects were exhaustive, including running financial metrics and calculating the effects of acquisitions and divestitures on the price of each company's stock.

After all this analysis Level 5 leadership proved to be one of the strongest, most consistent contrasts between the good-to-great and the comparison companies. Other factors transforming a company from good to great included getting the right people on the bus, and the wrong people off the bus, and creating a culture of discipline. Despite the contribution of these factors, the good-to-great transformations did not take place without Level 5 leadership.

The idea that humility combined with will facilitate leadership success in the firms that Collins studied fits the theme of this book. Humility made a big contribution but was not sufficient. For example, Darwin Smith at Kimberly-Clark also developed and executed excellent strategies. He concluded that the company's traditional core business of coated paper was doomed to mediocrity. Smith sold the company mills with all proceeds being thrown into the consumer business with investments in brands like Huggies diapers and Kleenex tissues. Level 5 leaders were described as demonstrating a compelling modesty, avoiding public adulation, and never being boastful. Yet they also had the cognitive skills to be good business strategists.

How the Level 5 Leaders Manifest Humility. The late Darwin Smith, who was CEO of Kimberly-Clark for 20 years was cited by Collins as the epitome of Level 5 leadership. Shy and awkward, Smith shunned attention, yet he also displayed iron will by redefining Kimberly-Clark's core business despite skepticism from Wall Street analysts. A mediocre performer for a long time, Kimberly-Clark became the world leader in its industry, generating stock returns 4.1 times greater than the average market return.

Considering that Level 5 leaders facilitated the success of their business enterprises it is worthwhile examining how they manifest humility. These leaders routinely credit others, external factors, and good luck as having contributed to the success of their companies. In contrast when results are poor, they blame themselves for having made poor decisions. Level 5 leaders also act quietly, calmly and with determination, and rely more on inspired standards than charisma to motivate others. Inspired standards illustrate the unwavering will of these leaders. Based on their intolerance of mediocrity, they are stoic in their resolve to do whatever is necessary to produce great results. With Darwin Smith that meant achieving greatness with even ordinary products such as Kleenex. (Nothing to sneeze at!) Level 5 leaders select strong successors, with a desire for their companies to become even more successful in the future.

HUMILITY AND IMPROVED DECISION-MAKING

Humility on the part of leaders and professionals can improve their decision-making. Improved decision-making can consequently improve individual, team, and organizational performance. As mentioned in Chapter 1, intellectually humble leaders are likely to gather multiple inputs before making a decision because they do not think they have all the answers. Intellectual humility contributes to more effective decisions because the leader or professional quickly absorbs and accurately evaluates input without being overly influenced by their own beliefs. Research by Mark Leary showed that when presented with facts, humble leaders did a better job of evaluating the quality of evidence, even on mundane matters.[11]

Leaders or professionals with intellectual humility recognize the fallibility of their beliefs and are less likely to dismiss people with different viewpoints or insult them for having a different opinion. Jud, the owner of a prosperous restaurant that featured barbeque-style food, decided the restaurant should perform a social good. He proposed to the supervisors of his kitchen and wait staff that he planned to offer jobs to released prisoners. The prisoners recruited would be those not convicted of violent crimes and would be screened for drug use and learning ability. Teena, the head of the wait staff blurted out, "Jud, you are losing your mind. The sweet little criminals you hire will rob us blind. When the public learns about what we are doing, we will lose half our customers."

Being intellectually humble, Jud replied, "I see your point Teena. Maybe I have overlooked something. But a few other restaurants have recruited prisoners with success. Let's a least give my program a chance." (Notice that intellectual humility, as with Jud, does not mean that a leader is always swayed by a contrary opinion. What intellectual humility does mean is that the leader or professional is able to accept criticism without retaliating and reflect on whether he or she was missing something.)

A HUMBLE LEADER WHO ACHIEVES EXTRAORDINARY RESULTS: ALPHABET AND GOOGLE CEO SUNDAR PICHAI

In 2014, Sundar Pichai became the CEO of Google, the major division of Alphabet, and became CEO of the parent company, Alphabet Inc. shortly thereafter. Under his leadership, Google has further entrenched its position as one of the most successful business enterprises of all time. Pichai is an unassuming man of humble beginnings, growing up with his parents and a brother in a two-room apartment in Chennai, India. Always brilliant, as shown in his ability to memorize hundreds of numbers dialed on a rotary phone, he was a reserved but fiercely competitive student.

Pichai has been described as the most powerful person in mobile, yet at the same time is known as a leader with strong humility. His leadership style has been described as self-deprecating, empathetic, and he is frequently referred to as "quiet," "shy," and "humble." His rise to Google CEO took 11 years, based on his technical knowledge, team player attitudes, and astuteness about office politics. Today, Pichai's main responsibility is to ensure that Google's core business and revenue, particularly advertising, stay strong.

Google co-founder Larry Page said of Pichai, "Sundar has a tremendous ability to see what's ahead and mobilize teams around the super important stuff." A former product manager at Google attributed part of Pichai's rise to power to having recruited, mentored, and retained a highly effective team. His team of product managers has a reputation for being the best of the best. He navigated office politics at Google to help his team be successful while not adversely affecting the other teams.

With respect to his focus on teams, Pichai says, "Nothing makes me happier than a product review in which I can sit with the team and they're showing me something they're building." People who work closely with Pichai comment favorably on his empathy, humor, and eagerness to encourage teamwork across Google. Pichai says his leadership style is a belief in the ability to transcend work and work well with others.

Soft-spoken and polite, Pichai supported whatever team he led, and ensured that the efforts of every team member were recognized by outsiders to the team. When attending team meetings. Pichai would usually sit at the back, listen quietly, and then after everyone else had spoken, present a collaborative idea. Ever since he has been at Google, Pichai has been well-liked. Because of his reputation of being enjoyable to work with, many Google professionals wanted to transfer to his organizational unit. It was therefore easier for Pichai to build strong teams.

Clay Bavor, the Google vice president of virtual and augmented reality, describes Pichai as a "deeply thoughtful, caring human person." Pichai's focus is on building the organization, not on being the center of attention. His conversational and personal style is relaxed and non-confrontational, helping to build relationships. Pichai's penchant for building relationships facilitates his implementing a collaborative leadership style.

Pichai may be humble, but his vision for Google is far-reaching. His stated goal is to give people everywhere the power of Google's machine learning (AI) whenever and wherever they need it.

The story about Pichai being a humble and effective leader does not mean that he and Google have not received considerable criticism. Almost all highly placed leaders face heavy criticism at some point in their careers. Here we mention several of the criticisms made of Pichai. Under Pichai's leadership, Google has been accused of not doing enough to protect user privacy, and not controlling the impact that Google has on the world. Attacks against the company can also be considered attacks against the CEO. In 2018, YouTube, a part of Google, was criticized for its abundance of divisive or misleading content.

Pichai's humble style of leadership is perceived by some people to be a shortcoming. In 2021, a report based on 15 current and former executives expressed concern about the amount of time Pichai takes to make decisions. Employees expressed frustration that Google did not move fast enough on major business decisions and personnel moves because Pichai ruminated over decisions and delayed action. For instance, several employees complained that Pichai took a year to fill a key position despite the availability of key candidates. The same group of employees mentioned that Google did not purchase Shopify as an example of Pichai's overly deliberate decision-making process.

During 2017–2018, Google was hit with several opposing lawsuits, arguing that the company was not doing enough or going too far in the push for diversity. Google received considerable criticism when James Damore, an engineer, was fired for writing a memo that argued women were biologically less interested in technology than men. Damore and three other employees sued the company for allegedly discriminating against white, conservative men. The lawsuit was later dropped. Pichai defended the firing saying that what Damore wrote did not fit the diversity culture of Google.

The market dominance of Google has created regulatory problems. In July 2017, the European Union fined Google $5 billion for abusing the dominance of its Android mobile operating system. Google has also been accused of suppressing conservative voices, but not to the extent that legal action against the company has yet been proposed. In January 2023, the US Justice Department and eight states filed a complaint against Alphabet's Google over allegations that the company abused its dominance of the digital advertising business. Later that same year, nine states joined the Justice lawsuit against Google.

Being a humble leader, Pichai listens to all the criticisms, weighs the evidence, and then decides if corrective action is required. For example, in response to the criticism raised in 2020 that Google was cutting back on diversity efforts, Pichai responded, "All I can say is that we probably have more resources invested in diversity now than at any point in our history as a company."[12]

GUIDELINES FOR ACTION

1. A useful framework for understanding leadership humility is that will often foster positive outcomes for the individual workers, organizational units, and the entire organization.

2. Humble leadership is well worth a try for facilitating creativity among group or team members, but the effect is indirect rather than direct. Humility by the leader creates an atmosphere of psychological safety, or one in which workers will risk proposing new ideas with fear of harsh criticism from co-workers.

3. Psychological safety can be developed by encouraging group members, appreciating their contributions, and building trust and supportive relationships with them. A caution is that psychological safety must be combined with knowledge sharing among group members for creativity to be enhanced.[13]

4. Humility can have a big payoff in terms of employee engagement. As a leader, if you establish a group climate in which people have the opportunity to learn and develop, group members will invest more of themselves in their jobs.

5. If you are a humble leader or professional you do not have to be brilliant in so many aspects of dealing with problems facing the group. Instead, you can also make use of the expertise within the group.

6. A key advantage of being a humble leader is that it encourages team and group members to become actively involved in solving problems facing the group. In contrast, leaders who think they have all the answers will tend to decrease the problem-solving activity within the group.

7. For leadership humility at the top of the organization to have a major impact it should be combined with intense personal will or passion. Expressed differently, as a leader you might respect the opinions of others, and appreciate their strengths. Yet at the same time you are driven to obtain good results for your organizational unit or the entire organization.

NOTES

1. Megan K. Johnson Wade C. Rowatt, and Leo Petrini, "A New Trait on the Market: Honesty-Humility as a Unique Predictor of Job Performance Ratings," *Personality and Individual Differences*, No 6, 2011, pp. 857–862.
2. Yanfei Wang Jiegiong Liu, and Yu Zhu, "Humble Leadership, Psychological Safety, Knowledge Sharing, and Follower Creativity: A Cross-Level Investigation," *Frontiers in Psychology* (ncbi.nlm.nih.gov), No 9, 2018, pp. 1–13.
3. Bradley P. Owens, Michael D. Johnson, and Terence Mitchell, "Expressed Humility in Organizations: Implications for Performance, Teams, and Leadership," *Organization Science*, September–October 2013, p. 1529.
4. Owens, Johnson, and Mitchell, "Expressed Humility in Organizations," p. 1533.
5. Antonio Argandona, "Humility in Management," *Springer* (published online August 7, 2014, p. 6).
6. Bradley P. Owens and Daniel Heckman, "How Does Leader Humility Influence Team Performance? Exploring the Mechanisms of Contagion and Collective Promotion Focus," *Academy of Management Journal*, June 2016, pp. 1088–1111; Sadie, O'Neil, Review of "How Leader Humility Boosts Team Performance," www.ioatwork.com, November 2, 2018, pp. 1–5.
7. Arménio Rego, Miguel Pina e Cunha and Ace Volkman Simpson, "The Perceived Impact of Leaders' Humility on Team Effectiveness: An Empirical Study," *Journal of Business Ethics* Volume 148, 2018, pp. 205–218.
8. Amy Y. Ou, David A. Waldman, and Suzanne J. Peterson, "Do Humble CEOs Matter? An Examination of CEO Humility and Firm Outcomes," *Journal of Management*, No 3, January 3, 2018, pp. 1147–1173.
9. Amy Y Ou et al, "Humble Chief Executives Officers' Connections to Top Management Team Integration and Middle Managers' Responses," *Administrative Science Quarterly*, January 8, 2014 (doi: 10.1177/0001839213520131); "How Humility in the CEO Improves Management Performance," *Ideas for Leaders* (info@idesfor leaders.com) Accessed May 21, 2020.
10. Jim Collins, *Good to Great: Why Some Companies Make the Leap … and Others Don't* (New York: Harper Business, 2001); Collins, "Level 5 Leadership: The Triumph of Humility and Fierce Resolve," *Harvard Business Review*, January 2001.
11. Mark R. Leary et al, "Cognitive and Interpersonal Features of Intellectual Humility," *Personality and Social psychology Bulletin*, March 17, 2017, doi: 10.1177/0146167217697695 pp. 1–16; Colleen Slaughter Rowe, "Intellectual Humility Can Make You a Better Leader," *Authentic Leadership International* (boldermoves.com), pp. 1–2.
12. Original story based on facts and observations in the following sources: "Leadership Lessons with Sundar Pichai," *UnStop* (www.unstop.com), September 28, 2021, pp. 1–3; "Google I/O 2016: 12 Leadership Qualities of Google's Sundar Pichai," *Digital Scribbler* (www.digitalscribbler.com), 2016, pp. 1–11; Adi Robertson, "Sundar Pichai Says Google has 'More Resources Invested in Diversity' than Ever After Reports of Cut Training Programs," *The Vergecast* (www.theverge.com), May 19, 2020, pp. 1–4; Jason Aten, "Google's CEO Is Facing Intense Criticism for His Leadership

His Response is Pure Emotional Intelligence," *Inc* (Inc.com), July 10, 2021, pp. 1–7; "Nine More US States Join Federal Lawsuit Against Google Over Ad Tech," *reuters .com*, April 17, 2023, p. 1.

13. Wang Liu, and Zhu, "Humble Leadership, Psychological Safety, Knowledge Sharing, and Follower Creativity," p. 12.

3

The Impact of Humility on Employee Behavior

An outstanding reason for a leader to express humility is that it can have a positive impact on employee behavior. Imagine that project manager Mia is discussing with team member Leo what can be done to shorten delivery time on a prototype for a device that extracts plastic waste from sea water. Leo has several suggestions, and asks Mia which suggestion will most likely work. Humble Mia responds, "Leo you have worked on these ideas for two weeks. With your new expertise, you tell me which of these three suggestions has the highest probability of speeding up delivery time." Leo thinks, "This is good stuff. My project manager regards me as a team expert on shortening delivery time. I feel much more confident now."

When this act of humility on the part of Mia is repeated with Leo as well as other team members, Mia facilitates the self-confidence of project team members. As shown in the figure below, a positive impact on employee behavior is important for the organization because behavior is in turn linked to performance. In the example with Mia and Leo, Leo develops more self-confidence because the humility Mia expresses helps him feel that his expertise is valued. In this chapter we describe a variety of positive behaviors that leadership and professional humility might enhance (Figure 3.1).

DOI: 10.4324/9781003461784-3

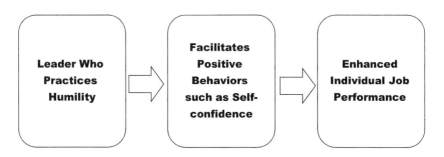

FIGURE 3.1 The relationship between employee behavior and performance.

GROUP MEMBERS MODELING HUMILITY

A key impact of humility on the part of a leader is that it often establishes a positive example for group members to model or follow. When a leader admits to his or her mistakes and takes actions that benefit the greater good, such behavior creates an atmosphere of promoting group goals. Modeling usually does not involve telling group members how to behave, but instead provides an opportunity for others to emulate what appears to be effective or appropriate behavior. Here are two examples of modeling as revealed by interview responses in a research study:[1]

Modeling Behavior	Example in Action
Acknowledging limitations and mistakes	*Comment by the leader*: "I made a business decision when I initiated something, went forward, and then received feedback that the initiative was not working. I then said, 'You know what? I messed up. We need to redo this.' I tried to be upfront and admit that I made a mistake, and that we needed to try again."
Spotlighting group member strengths and contributions	*Comment by a group member*: "We had an incredibly complex project that was delivered as a huge success. The leader gave everybody on the team all the credit." *Comment by another group member*: "When the team had a big success, he made sure the person who did the work received the recognition. He will make sure the person gets noticed."

Leadership humility can also be a good model for how the leader's direct reports deal with their own staff. The idea is that many leaders acquire leadership behaviors by observing how they are treated by their own bosses. Imagine that Larry, the president of the battery division of an automotive supply company, explains to his staff that the division will be facing a serious cash-flow problem for the final two quarters of the fiscal year. Larry says that he is worried about the problem but he believes strongly that his staff will generate a few creative ideas to help reduce the cash-flow problem. He then asks the staff to begin thinking about the problem, and that he looks forward to receiving their suggestions.

One of the comments Larry makes during the meeting is "A cash-flow shortfall is a problem that can affect the livelihood of our entire division. We therefore have to solve the problem together." Larry has therefore served as a model of humility for his staff. When his top-management team (the staff members) face a difficult problem, they will be more likely to tap the expertise of their own groups.

INSPIRED EMPLOYEES

Inspired employees are important for organizational health for several reasons as revealed by the HOW report, a long-term research project on organizational effectiveness, behavior, and leadership. Inspired workers demonstrate several characteristics. They are authentically dedicated in the sense of being proud of their organization for how it acts in the work. As a result, these inspired workers are self-driven, and hold themselves accountable. They accept authority for problems, and meet their obligations. Furthermore, they are good organizational citizens in terms of helping others. The characteristics just mentioned translate into inspired employees being much more productive than non-inspired employees.[2]

Inspirational leadership is often attributed to a leader's positive traits and behavior such as being extraverted, charismatic, and colorful. Yet inspiration is also fostered by traits and behaviors associated with humility. Being listened to carefully can be inspirational because the worker is likely to believe that he or she has ideas of merit. Consciously or pre-consciously, the worker might think, "This is really good. My boss thinks I have useful ideas to contribute. I'll keep trying to generate more useful ideas."

A humble leader will often inspire employees by treating them with dignity and respect. Workers who perceive that they are considered worthy of respect will often be motivated to perform at their best. (We use the qualifier *often* because no single aspect of leadership humility will work well with all employees all the time.)

The compassion component of humility can be inspiring for many employees. When you believe that your leader is strongly concerned about your problems, and combines concern with compassion, you might be inspired to elevate your performance. Kelly, an assistant bank manager, provides an example. She and her husband and two children were the victims of a house fire that created chaos and trauma.

The emotionally draining and time-consuming activities included moving to a temporary relocation, purchasing new clothing and home furnishings, and documenting losses for the insurance company. For the first four weeks after the fire, it was difficult for Kelly to concentrate on work. Not only did Charlotte, the bank manager, express deep sympathy for Kelly's plight, she was granted a week of paid leave to deal with fire-related problems.

In response to Charlotte's treatment of her during the personal crisis, Kelly commented,

> I am so grateful to the bank and Charlotte in particular. After our personal situation calmed down, I dug harder than ever into my job. I wanted to prove that the kindness showed me was a good investment for the bank and Charlotte.

Perhaps the most inspirational facet of humble leadership is transcendence. Humble leaders tame their ego and embrace a leadership perspective that seeks to elevate everyone. When workers throughout the organization see that the highest-ranking leader wants to help everybody else succeed, including earning more money, the workers will be inspired to perform at their best.

FOSTERING PROACTIVE BEHAVIOR

Slightly less grandiose than inspired behavior but still important is proactivity. Proactive workers are inclined to engage in such behaviors as seeking feedback, going beyond their job description, taking the initiative to engage in job-relevant learning, and going out to meet customers. The opposite of proactive is to be reactive, such as reacting to flood damage by cleaning up rather than being reactive and preventing flood damage through reinforced basement walls. The proactive worker is self-starting, geared toward the future, and attempts to bring about change in himself or herself or change the situation. At the same time, proactive workers fix problems without being told what to do.

Why does humble leadership foster proactive behavior among group members? A subtle link between humble leadership and proactive employee behavior is that humble leaders are more likely to hire proactive employees because humble leaders welcome talent. In contrast, a leader with a strong ego might be concerned about adding a team member to the group who will take so much initiative, and contribute so many good ideas, that the leader's role will diminish in importance.

A humble leader is likely to favor job candidates who have a demonstrated record of proactivity, such as having volunteered good ideas for cost-cutting or process improvement. Such behaviors will sometimes be revealed through skilled interviewing or reference checking. An example of a specific method of employee selection that is likely to find proactive employees is the hiring of *asset employees*, as described by Matthew Beecher.[3] An asset employee refers to a person who is most likely to improve the organization, a primary characteristic of the proactive worker. A hiring manager with humility would focus on the strengths and skills of the applicant that may enhance a specific department.

Beecher emphasizes that average employees typically meet job requirements but choose not to exceed them. Although they may have strengths that could propel them toward superior performance, they lack the motivation to capitalize on these strengths. In contrast, the best employees are assets because they exceed their pay grade in value and contributions. Being proactive, asset employees continually improve the organization. These employees use their talents to correct inefficiencies and reduce expenses. At the same time, they strengthen the organizational culture by fostering teamwork and respect for a strong work ethic.

A manager or leader with a strong dose of humility will welcome all these qualities he or she is not seeking to be the standout performer. Similarly, a corporate professional welcomes an asset employee as a teammate. Here are three interview questions, the answers to which might prove useful in detecting proactive behavior.

- At your previous job, how important was your role in helping the company make a profit?
- How have your personal strengths directly improved your prior places of employment?
- What are two problems you worked on in the past without the prompting of your boss?

The interview observations should be supplemented with discussions with prior managers and co-workers about the candidate's use of strengths and initiative taking. Quite often such information is difficult to attain because of privacy issues, and the concerns many people have about the legal implications of saying something negative about a former employee. Even if these legal concerns are unfounded in a particular state or province, many managers are still hesitant to make negative statements about any former employee.

The constant learning dimension of humble leadership is another contributor to employee proactivity, mostly through modeling. As mentioned in Chapter 1, self-awareness inspires the leader to constantly improve to acquire more advanced skills. Acquiring these skills requires a proactive approach to deciding which skills and abilities will be needed in the future. If group members see that looking to acquire skills that might be needed in the future is valued, they might be proactive enough to do the same. For example, perhaps Malcolm, a retirement specialist in a bank, has not yet been told to learn about how cyber currencies might become part of retirement planning. Yet because his boss is a proactive learner, Malcolm might take the initiative to learn about the future impact of cyber currencies on retirement planning.

ENHANCED COLLABORATION

The humble style of leadership encourages collaboration among group members themselves and with the leader for several reasons. A leader with humility values information sharing because the leader recognizes that he or she does not possess all the relevant exercise to tackle major problems. As explained by leadership coaches Jenny Fernandez and Luis Velasquez, success is not having the final word or getting your way. Instead, the leader consults other group members with the information needed to solve the problem. This approach to information sharing leads naturally to collaboration within the group because sharing information is the heart of collaboration.[4]

Emily, a wealth management adviser in a financial services firm, has a client interested in investing in an exotic investment, futures in the price of bitcoin. She therefore collaborates with Jack, a bitcoin specialist, to help the client with the investment. Collaboration through information sharing can also involve multiple members of the group, such as four members of the wealth management group sharing their knowledge about bitcoin futures.

Part of the same reason that humble leaders and professionals prefer to collaborate on problems is that they recognize that they are not experts with respect to all the problems they face. A potent example of this reality is that when an IT support technician is working on a client's baffling problem with software or hardware, the technician often does a Google search to find the answer—right in front of the client! The IT technician is humble enough to admit not having the appropriate expertise to solve the problem, and consults some other anonymous expert out there in the cloud. At a group level, as a leader shows a willingness to borrow expertise, group members model the approach.

The modesty dimension of humility also facilitates collaboration. Modesty allows for letting other people be in the spotlight, when group members collaborate with each other, they tend to share being placed in the spotlight. The modest leader sets an example that modesty is favorable behavior. In turn the modest group member is more prone to collaborate with others to obtain their input on out-of-the-ordinary problems.

A humble leader might be effective in fostering collaboration, but he or she should also be aware of the potential dysfunctions of collaboration. Teamwork and collaboration can have diminishing returns. Over the past two decades, the time spent by managers and employees in collaborative activities has surged by at least 50 percent. Most managerial workers spend at least 85 percent of their work time in email, meetings, and on the phone. The need for collaboration has been attributed to the increased complexity of products and services, globalization, digital messaging, and the widespread use of collaborative tools and digital messaging.

When demands for collaboration and teamwork are excessive, workflow bottlenecks and employee burnout often occur. For example, too much time spent in meetings, or conversing with co-workers may make it difficult for some workers to complete analytical and creative work.[5]

FEELINGS OF EMPOWERMENT

A noted strength of leadership humility is that it facilitates feelings of empowerment among group and team members. Because humility includes depending on other people, it lends itself to empowerment. The humble leader communicates the idea that, "You are in the best position to deal with this problem, so I authorize you to decide what is best, and execute the solution."

Rick, a hotel manager with humility, might encourage the receptionists to deal with guests' complaints the best they can within limits. A receptionist might be dealing with an angry guest who said that guests in the next room fighting most of the night disturbed her sleep. With a humble leader, the receptionist might really believe she can give the guest a 25 percent reduction on the bill as compensation for her disturbed sleep. If Rick were not at all humble, the receptionist might think Rick would be disturbed by her generosity.

Humble leaders empower others to learn and grow by acknowledging that they do not have all the answers, and therefore the knowledge contributions of others will be needed now and into the future. Expressed differently, group members might think, "My knowledge is needed to keep our group functioning at a high level. And other job-related knowledge I pick up might be needed in the future."

Richard Branson, the flamboyant British entrepreneur who built the Virgin empire, is certainly not humble in his public self. Yet his attitudes toward running an enterprise (rather than promoting it) reflect humility. Branson observes that to build a successful venture, entrepreneurs must have self-confidence, dynamism, and tenacity. Yet they shift to a humbler leadership style when they recognize they need help in running the enterprise. Shifting from "self" to "less self" is a critical part of the transition that empowers a team and enables the organization to run efficiently and effectively. Branson writes that the entrepreneur's job is to basically put himself or herself out of a job when the new company is up and running.[6] Much humility is needed to put oneself out of a job.

Another way in which humility by a leader fosters empowerment is by giving employees a say or *voice* with respect to their work. Voice behavior is the extent to which workers speak up toward authority, offer constructive suggestions for change, and challenge the status quo with the intent of making improvements. Speaking up is a form of empowerment because team members are given the opportunity to influence decision-making and work activities based on their ability to raise concerns and solve problems. Humble leaders encourage employee voice because they welcome input into decisions as well as suggestions for improvement.

A study conducted in the Netherlands by Sanni Kluitenberg investigated the mechanism by which humble leadership encourages voice among team members. The study participants were 209 team members from 52 teams in 21 companies. An overall conclusion reached was that humble leadership is positively associated with team members expressing their voice. The key influencing (or mediating) factor was the leader freely exchanging information with team members.

When team members readily exchanged information with the leader, they were more likely to feel they had a voice. A key part of the information exchange is for the leader to be open to new ideas and information which makes him or her receptive to feedback. Listening before speaking to group members is another part of information exchange. Instead of telling followers what to do, he or she listens and develops work processes and solutions together.[7]

Heightened Self-Confidence

At their best, leaders with the right amount of humility help group members strengthen their self-confidence.[8] The reason is that self-confidence ordinarily develops as a result of the accumulation of small victories. Because the humble leader is not searching for ways to impress others and take credit for most group accomplishments, he or she will often make a statement such as, "That's a good idea. Go ahead and give it a try." If the idea the group member tries, and it is successful, he or she will have a small gain in self-confidence. As the same person successfully implements more suggestions he or she was encouraged to try, the person's self-confidence will continue to grow, a small increment at a time.

A direct way in which a humble leader enhances the self-confidence of group members is through acknowledging their strengths. Such behavior is one of the bedrock characteristics of a leader with humility. Imagine the situation of Megan, the sales manager at a garment manufacturer. She receives an angry email from a store owner saying that he has received six complaints that the yoga pants we shipped him fall apart during strenuous exercise. Megan gets on the phone with Abigail, the customer support manager. Being a humble leader (or a deft delegator), she says to Abigail, "You're better at calming down customers and solving their problems than me. How would you like to tackle this problem for us?" Whether or not Abigail can resolve this problem, her self-confidence has increased a little because Megan has told that she is talented in dealing with angry customers.

Humble leaders can also lift the collective self-confidence of group members by emphasizing the importance of each member's contribution. The effect is not guaranteed, but being told that you are a valued team member can result in a small self-confidence boost.

The bulleted list that follows suggests behaviors and actions of a humble leader that can be helpful in boosting the self-confidence of group members. Using a variety or combination of these behaviors and actions will be more effective than relying on just one.

- Points to a specific contribution of a group member, such as "Karl you really nailed a process for reducing our inventory."
- Points out that someone else on the team is the expert on a specific subject not him or her, such as "Niki is our resident expert on setting up a Zoom meeting, and I have no first-hand knowledge on how to do it. So, she will be in charge of setting up the meeting."
- Encourages a group member to build a complex skill, a little step at a time, such as, "Calvin, I know that you are just getting started programming robots. I would like you as a first step to get this robot to move parts along the assembly line."
- Tells the group during a physical or virtual meeting, "I'm the idea-collector in-chief. Without your collective expertise our department could never carry out its mission."
- CEO says to the top-management team, "I will be away next Monday through Wednesday at a strategy retreat. Most likely, you will not even notice I am gone."
- Says to a financial analyst who just finished a thorough report on how changes in the values of major currencies around the world might impact profitability for the next two quarters, "I am so proud of you for providing us this fantastic report."
- Says to his or her executive assistant, "I couldn't do this job without your support."

A caveat here is that there are limits to the impact of leadership humility on self-confidence. A team member with a deeply ingrained self-confidence problem is not likely to become more confident just because the leader takes the actions stated in the bulleted list.

ENHANCED RESILIENCE

Humble leadership also contributes to facilitating employee resilience. Resilient employees cope, adapt, and even thrive in response to dynamic and challenging environments. The humble leader might act as a model for dealing with difficult problems, such as losing a major customer. Leadership humility also converts crises into developmental challenges which provides an intellectual challenge to help employees cope with the situation. For example, a humble leader might point out that a new product failed during its first field test, but that does not mean the product is doomed. What it does mean is the group has to find a way to correct the problems.[8]

Two Pathways to Resilience

A study conducted in Mainland China investigated how humble leadership may catalyze employee resistance through two pathways. (The reason so much of the empirical research about humility has been conducted in China is that the country's culture places a high value on humility.)

The first pathway studied was *work-related promotion focus*. A person with such a focus would actively pursue gains or advancement. He or she would also strive to minimize the discrepancy between the actual and ideal states, such as thinking, "This software is user-unfriendly. It jumps around so much that many users would become frustrated. I want to fix this problem." The individual with a work-related promotion focus would also be sensitive to the presence or absence of positive outcomes, such as "How come this new packaging machine we just listed for sale is drawing so few inquiries," or "Why is this new packaging machine we just listed for sale getting so many inquiries?"

Two sample questionnaire items used to measure work-related promotion focus were as follows: "I take chances at work to maximize my goals for advancement," and "I spend a great deal of time envisioning how to fulfill my aspirations."

The second pathway studied in this research was *perceived insider identity*. As implied by the term, perceived insider identity refers to the extent to which an employee perceives himself or herself to be an insider within the organization. An employee who feels like an insider is more likely to be committed to the organization and experience work engagement. When you feel like an insider you are also more likely to take a proactive approach to problem-solving.

Two sample questionnaire items to measure perceived insider identity were as follows: "I feel very much part of my work organization," and "My work organization makes me feel included in it."

The major finding of the study was that humble leadership increased employee work-related promotion focus as well as perceived insider identity. In turn, workers having increased promotion focus and perceived insider identity tended to be more resilient. Leadership humility therefore sets up conditions associated with better resilience. Digging deeper into the results, the aspects of humility that enhanced promotion focus and perceived insider identity were having an objective self-evaluation, openness to new ideas, and showing appreciation for the thoughts of employees.[9] (These are three basic components of leadership humility.)

Psychological Capital and Resilience. Another link between leadership humility and resilience is that humble leadership fosters psychological capital among group members.[10] Psychological capital entails hope, efficacy, resilience and optimism, and all four are intertwined with self-confidence. In more detail, the components of psychological capital are as follows:

- *Hope* refers to persevering toward goals, and when necessary, redirecting paths to a goal in order to succeed.
- *Self-efficacy* refers to having the confidence to take on and invest the necessary effort to succeed at challenging tasks. Experience is a big help here, because if you have successfully completed the same task, or a similar one, previously, you will be more confident that you can succeed.
- *Optimism* refers to making a positive attribution about succeeding now and in the future. If you are a natural pessimist you will have to work harder at looking for the positive aspects of a given situation.
- *Resiliency* refers to dealing with problems and adversity by sustaining effort and bouncing back to attain success. Conquering a major setback would be an enormous contributor to your self-confidence.[11]

Fostering psychological capital comes about in part because the leader gives subordinates room to grow and develop, and frequently points to their strengths. Furthermore, the humble leader sees setbacks as a necessary part of the developmental process. Because humble leaders do not try to keep up appearances or act powerful, it is less distressing for group members and therefore easier to receive when facing a job setback, such as a failed project.

COPING WITH A CRISIS SUCH AS THE PANDEMIC

The positive impact of leadership humility on employee behavior was demonstrated during the pandemic. Discussions with a handful of CEOs revealed that humility was the one leadership trait that stood out in getting workers through the pandemic. The finding is not surprising because leaders who incorporate humility into their leadership style take the opinions of workers seriously, encourage them to express their feelings, and foster trust and collaboration.

Alex Zhu and Jonathan Smith, who interviewed the CEOs just mentioned, observed that during the unexpected challenge of the pandemic, the leaders actively sought out the opinions of group members. The empathy aspect of humility emerged as a key theme in helping workers get through the crisis because it provided a sense of togetherness and collective resilience. The sense of togetherness and collective resilience, in turn, helped employees respond to challenges with an enhanced sense of solidarity and grit.[12]

Michelle Gass, the CEO of Kohl's, is an example of how empathy helped workers get through the pandemic. During the height of the pandemic, all the company stores were closed temporarily, and 80,000 of the company's 100,000 employees were furloughed. Gass and her executive team established two priorities: maintaining the financial health of the company and ensuring the health and safety of Kohl's employees and the company's customers. Gass commented that the fundamental principles of great leadership are "humanity, empathy, and being courageous."[13] (Note that humanity and empathy are key components of humility.)

RESPECT FOR THE LEADER AND THE ORGANIZATION

Garnering respect for the leader, and subsequently for the organization, is an impact of considerable value. Being respected helps a leader be listened to by group members. Respect for the organization leads to such positive outcomes as lower employee turnover and more referrals to the organization with respect to recruits and customers.

A key humble leadership behavior that brings respect is openness to the opinion of others. Humble leaders ask for input from others to ensure that they have all the relevant facts and are making decisions that are in the best interest of the team. People prefer to report to a manager who values their opinions, rather than brushing off their ideas. Even if the leader arrives at a decision different than the group, he or she is respected for having consulted the members. During a crisis a humble leader might be expected to take decisive action, and he or she earns the respect of the group because of having consulted the members.

Admitting mistakes is another important way in which a leader earns the respect of group members. Because the leader is often a worker's key contact with the organization, the respect for the leader will often generalize to respect for the entire organization. Leaders who share their missteps with the group, and explain how they recovered, gain both respect and trust.[14] Here is an example: Plant manager Brett says to his management team,

> *I got into some trouble with corporate. I said we could deliver our new model industrial sanitizer by the 15th of this month. We are at least three weeks behind. My mistake was not taking into account supply chain disturbances in getting the parts that we needed. I explained how the mistake happened, and that we would establish backup suppliers in the future.*

Another way in which humble leaders gain respect is by building supportive relationships with subordinates. Leaders with high levels of humility usually avoid being competitive with others in a zero-sum game, and also avoid disrespectful behaviors such as ridiculing, interrupting, or coercing others. As a result, they are likely to develop supportive relationships with their employees.[15]During a physical or virtual meeting, a supportive leader who doubts the usefulness of a team member's suggestion is likely to make a respectful comment, such as "Have you thought of this potential negative consequence of your otherwise good suggestion?" The questioning of the team member's suggestion, rather than making an insulting comment, generates respect.

Work Engagement and Service-Minded Employees

We previously mentioned that humble leadership can impact employee engagement in a positive way. Another wrinkle is that engagement can also be accompanied by a stronger commitment to service. A study was conducted in Norway with 1,500 leaders and their employees that explored the influence of transformational and humble leadership behaviors. Data were collected in both a financial services company and an audit company. The researchers demonstrated that leaders with good self-insight, who are humble, and act as credible role models are rewarded with committed and service-minded employees. (Note that having good self-insight and being a good role model can be regarded as part of leader humility.)

The leaders were asked to assess their own leadership style, and direct reports were also asked to assess their leader's style. Next, the researchers compared the employees' assessment with the leader's assessment of his or her style. Quite often there was a discrepancy between the leader's self-assessment and the assessment by the direct reports. When the employees perceive the leader to have a transformational style (brings about positive changes), it has a positive effect on work commitment and the perceived service climate. The impact on the service climate and engagement was the strongest when the leader was humble. A leader was classified as "humble" when he or she had a lower opinion of his or her leadership effectiveness than did the direct reports.[16]

HIGHER EMPLOYEE RETENTION

A strategic goal of human resources management is to reduce voluntary turnover, or encourage employees who meet or exceed performance standards to stay with the organization. When useful employees leave the firm, production and services are often interrupted. Furthermore, replacing good employees is time-consuming and expensive. Employee involuntary turnover and retention are both closely linked to leadership and management. When employees have a poor relationship with their manager, or dislike the person, they are more likely to quit. Conversely, when employees have a good relationship with their manager, or like the person, they are more likely to stay with the organization.

Leaders who are humble, and also competent in other ways, are more likely to retain employees. One of hundreds of possible examples of being "competent in other ways" is that many people, especially early in their careers, want to work for a leader who has good knowledge of the business and is a creative thinker. Working for such a knowledgeable leader gives the person an opportunity to grow and develop professionally.

Leadership humility contributes to higher retention and lower involuntary turnover because the leader establishes a comfortable working environment for employees. Humble leaders also are usually perceived as likable. The humble leader focuses more on the needs of workers and less on himself or herself. A leader who is too self-serving and narcissistic might convey the impression to subordinates that they are working to make him or her succeed and look good. In contrast, a leader with humility will usually generate the impression that he or she is working hard to make group members succeed and look good. When career-minded workers feel they have an opportunity to succeed, they are more likely to want to stay with the firm.

A LEADER WITH HUMILITY: TARA COMONTE, CEO OF TMRW, AND FORMER PRESIDENT AND CFO OF SHAKE SHACK

In 2021 Shake Shack president and CFO Tara Comonte was named chief executive officer of TMRW Life Sciences Inc., an integrated platform for *in-vitro* fertilization management. She had held a board seat at TMRW since the company began in 2018. Comonte was a hard-driving and talented executive at Shake Shack and also a leader with humility whose actions often have a positive impact on employees. The company mission is to Stand for Something Good®. In 2019, Comonte was promoted from chief financial officer to the expanded role of president and CFO. As president, Comonte focused on expanding the company, broadening support of day-to-day operations, and executing strategy. At the same time, she oversaw finance, accounting, technology, internal audit, and the legal department.

Comonte joined Shake Shack in 2017, and played a key role in the company's digital innovation, as well as providing direction to the enterprise-wide technology upgrade. She also has worked on Shake Shack's diversity and inclusion initiatives. Being involved in providing leadership in so many specialty areas, Comonte freely asked for advice and assistance from specialists in different business functions.

Comonte displayed her humility when she worked the grill on her first day on the job in a graceful, pleasant manner. (We give her some humility credit here, but every new employee regardless of job title, has to spend some of his or her training period in a restaurant at different stations. The aim is to learn how to make burgers, fries, and milkshakes.) A stronger display of humility is that during her time with the company, Comonte continued to spend time at the stores to get insight into what processes can be centralized to increase efficiency. A less humble approach would have been to have to data sent to her office instead of making in-person visits to the stores.

Randy Garutti, CEO of Shake Shack, made this comment about Comonte, "In addition to excellence in her field, Tara's commitment to diversity and inclusion, empowerment, and accountability are core to the very special culture we have here at Shake Shack."[17]

GUIDELINES FOR ACTION

1. Practicing humble leadership can be quite important for the organization because it has a positive impact on behaviors that, in turn, enhance individual and job performance. The impact of humble leadership can therefore be to trigger behaviors that lead to and sustain high performance.
2. Leadership humility can have a payoff by working as a model for staff members to be humble in their dealings with others. Assume that you are a middle manager with supervisors as direct reports, and you show humility in dealing with them. The supervisors are likely to model your humility in the way they deal with their direct reports.

3. Leadership humility can be effective in inspiring employees by listening to them, treating them with dignity and respect, and showing compassion.

4. A subtle contribution of a humble leader is his or her willingness to hire proactive workers because the leader welcomes rather than feels competitive with high performers.

5. Humble leadership can lead to enhanced collaboration because he or she imparts the value of information sharing. Unless group members are willing to share information, their collaboration will be limited.

6. Humble leadership is well-suited to empowerment because humility includes depending on people. When you depend on others, you are more likely to give them freedom to make decisions on their own.

7. As a humble leader you are in a good position to develop the self-confidence of group members because you give them the opportunity to experience a series of small wins.

8. Leadership humility can be effective in helping employees develop resilience. The humble leader might act as a role model for resilience. Helping group members feel that they are insiders, might make them feel more committed to overcoming workplace problems.

9. A key humble leadership behavior that brings respect to the leader and the organization is openness to the opinions of others.

10. Leadership humility contributes to higher retention and lower involuntary turnover because the leader establishes a comfortable working relationship for group members. A key part of a comfortable working relationship is that a humble leader is likable.

NOTES

1. Bradley P. Owens and David R. Hekman, "Modeling How to Grow: An Inductive Examination of Humble Leader Behaviors, Contingencies, and Outcomes," *Academy of Management Journal*, August 2012, pp. 798-799.
2. Michael Eichenwald, "The Importance of Inspirational Leadership," *Chief Learning Officer* (www.chieflearningofficer.com), February 27, 2017, p. 1.
3. Matthew Beecher, "Only Assets Need Apply," *HR Magazine*, November 2011, pp. 84-85.

4. Jenny Fernandez and Luis Velasquez, "Becoming More Collaborative When You Like to Be in Control," *Harvard Business Review* (https://hbr.org), March 23, 2023, p. 4.
5. "Too Much Togetherness? The Downside of Workplace Collaboration," *Knowledge@ Wharton* (www.knowledge.wharton.upenn.edu), November 9, 2019, pp. 1-7.
6. Bronson cited in Donna Grande, "The Imperative of Humble Leadership," *American Nurse Today*, March 2018, pp. 1-3.
7. Sanni Kluitenberg, "Humble Leadership and Team Voice," Master's Thesis, Maastricht University, January 2015.
8. Don Emerson Davis Jr., and Joshua N. Hook, "Measuring Humility and it Positive Effects," *Association for Psychological Science* (www.pscyhologicalscience.org). October 2013, pp. 1-6.
9. Yanhan Zhu, Shuwei Zhang, and Yomo Shen, "Humble Leadership and Employee Resilience: Exploring the Mediating Mechanism of Work-Related Promotion Focus and Perceived Insider Humility," *Frontiers in Psychology* (www.frontiersinpsycho logy.org), April 3, 2019, pp. 1-17.
10. Jamie Aten, "How Humble Leaders Foster Resilience: An Interview with Dr. Bradley Owens on the Value of Humility," *Psychology Today* (www.psychologytoday.com), February 26, 2019, pp. 1-3.
11. Fred Luthans, James R. Avey, and Jaime L. Patera, "Experimental Analysis of a Web-Based Training Intervention to Develop Positive Psychological Capital," *Academy of Management Learning and Education*, June 2008, pp. 209-221.
12. Alex Zhu and Jonathan Smith, "Leadership in a Covid-19 World: The Power of Humility," www.spencerstuart.com, May 14, 2020, pp. 1-2.
13. Cited in Ellie Austin, "The Lessons Kohl's Leadership Learned in the Pandemic," *The Wall Street Journal,* February 2021, p. A11.
14. Comments from Arron Grow Cited in Gwen Moran, "6 Ways Humility Can Make You a Better Leader," www.fastcompany.com, August 11, 2014, p. 1.
15. J. Andrew Morris, Céleste M. Brotheridge and John C. Urbanski, "Bringing Humility to Leadership: Antecedents and Consequences of Leader Humility," *Human Relations*, No. 10, 2005, p. 1341.
16. Karoline Kopperud, Øyvind L. Martinsen, and Sut I. Wong, "Engaging Leaders in the Eyes of the Beholder: On the Relationship Between Transformational Leadership, Work Engagement, Service Climate, and Self-Other Agreement," *Journal of Leadership and Organizational Studies,* February 2014.
17. Original story based on facts and observations in the following sources: "Tara Comonte: CEO at TMRW Life Sciences," Orgio Inc. (theorg.com), © 2023, pp. 1; Anny Stych, "Shake Shack President Named CEO of In Vitro Management Platform TMRW," *bizwoman* (www.bizwoman.com), March 32, 2021, pp. 1-3; "Shake Shack Promotes Tara Comonte to Expanded Role of President and Chief Financial Officer," *Shake Shack* (https://investor.shakeshack.com), October 2, 2019, pp. 1-3; Frances Bridges, "Shake Shack CFO Tara Comonte's Career Advice for Aspiring Leaders," *Forbes* (www.forbes.com), August 29, 2019, pp. 1-6; Sam Danley, "Shake Shack C.F.O. Promoted toPresident," *Food Business News* (www.foodbusinessnews .net), October 2, 2019, pp. 1-2. Rheaa Rao, "Burger Chain To Serve Up Changes," *The Wall Street Journal*, July 8, 2017, p. B5.

4

The Attributes of Humble Leaders and Professionals

Many of the actions and behaviors we have described about humble leaders and professional workers point toward their attributes or personal qualities. For example, if humble leader Quincy carefully assesses the strengths of team members, he is doing so partially because he is motivated to help others. If humble wealth adviser Ava listens carefully to the financial concerns of her client, she is doing so partly because she has empathy.

Attributes related to humility are worth looking at carefully because they are capable of development. With careful attention and practice, you can probably strengthen yourself with respect to these attributes. The attribute of mindfulness provides a good example. People can learn to become more mindful by carefully focusing on the moment at hand and minimizing distractions. If you can focus on the person talking to you, and not become diverted by your own thoughts or a small screen, you will be acting with humility toward that person.

We organize our description of the attributes related to humility into two loose categories. The first category is attributes related more to the self, and include personality traits. The second category is interaction with others. A *loose* category here refers to the idea that an argument could be made that a given attribute might also fit the other category. For example, mindfulness might be classified as a personal attribute yet it also involves interaction with others. We use the two categories to help organize the information into understandable chunks of information.

DOI: 10.4324/9781003461784-4

ATTRIBUTES RELATED MORE TO THE SELF

A humble leader or professional has many personal attributes that facilitate being humble. A handful of the key attributes are described next that would help a leader or professional be humble in many different situations.

Enthusiasm, Optimism, and Warmth. In almost all leadership situations it is desirable for leaders to be optimistic. Optimism helps build teamwork because it helps establish a climate in which it is enjoyable to work together. Team members tend to respond positively to enthusiasm, partly because enthusiasm may be perceived as a reward for constructive behavior. Humble leaders with their focus on others, tend to be highly enthusiastic when the team performs well.

Enthusiasm is also a highly desirable leadership trait because it helps build good relationships with team members. A leader can express enthusiasm both verbally ("Amazing job"; "I love it") and nonverbally (making an elbow bump or high-five gesture). Kevin A. Plank, the founder and CEO of Under Armour, is known for his hand-clapping style of enthusiasm. Plank does not always display humility but he can be humble at times, such as in talking about the accomplishments of his employees.

Enthusiasm often takes the form of optimism, which helps keep the team in an upbeat mood and hopeful about attaining difficult goals. The optimistic leader is therefore likely to bring about exceptional levels of achievement, particularly when he or she focuses the optimism on the team.

Being a warm person and projecting that warmth is part of enthusiasm and contributes to leadership effectiveness in several ways. First, warmth helps to establish rapport with group members. Second, emotional support helps provide emotional support to group members. Third, being warm is engaging, whereas being cold tends to create distance from others. Fourth, the projection of warmth is a component of charisma. Charismatic leaders are typically not regarded as humble, but they can be humble when they also express pride in the accomplishments of others.

Eagerness to Learn. Humble people understand the limits of their own knowledge, and are therefore eager to learn, or acquire new knowledge. This trait has also been referred to as intellectual humility. People with this attribute exhibit these behaviors:

- Acknowledge the limits of their own knowledge;
- Listen carefully to new ideas and criticisms;
- Willing to assess new sources of evidence;
- Receptive to acquiring new skills;
- Engage in constructive discourse.[1]

A person's fundamental view of intelligence can hinder his or her eagerness to learn, or intellectual humility. The long-term research of Stanford psychologist Carol Dweck indicates there are two types of mindsets. People with a *fixed mindset* believe that everyone is born with a certain level of intelligence, and because of this reality there is little point in trying to improve your problem-solving ability. They tend to believe that their talents are innate gifts. A person with a fixed mindset and who is highly intelligent, might be arrogant, and think that they do not need to acquire new knowledge.

People with a *growth mindset* view intelligence as something more malleable, such as a muscle that can be strengthened. A person with a growth mindset is therefore eager to learn, and has a humble view of his or her own intelligence.[2] The person believes that it is possible to develop his or her talents through hard work, good strategies, and input from others.

The person who is eager to learn will express doubt that he or she has the best solution to a problem, and will therefore be willing to learn from others.[3] Ashley, the company HR manager, might tell the other members of the top-management team that she thinks an effective way of attracting top talent to the firm would be to offer a remote-work option of two days per week. Thinking that her idea is sound, and based on the experience of other companies, Ashley still is humble enough to have some doubts. As a result, she says to the other managers, "What is your opinion of the two days of remote-work option to attract talent? I welcome your input."

Self-Confidence. Self-confidence improves one's performance in a variety of tasks including leadership. A leader who is self-assured without being bombastic or overbearing instills self-confidence in team members. Self-confidence was among the first leadership traits researchers identified, and it still receives considerable attention as a contributor to leadership effectiveness. The accompanying self-quiz offers you an opportunity to think about your level of self-confidence.

A humble leader stays in the middle of the continuum between self-confidence and arrogance. Self-confidence enters the picture because a person needs to feel secure and confident to recognize his or her limitations and to appreciate the strengths of others. You need self-confidence to surround yourself with capable, talented people. If you were not confident, you would feel inferior. At the other end of the continuum, an arrogant person is the antithesis of being humble.

HOW SELF-CONFIDENT ARE YOU?

Indicate the extent to which you agree with each of the following statements. Use a 1-to-5 scale: (1) *Disagree strongly*; (2) *Disagree*; (3) *Neutral*; (4) *Agree*; (5) *Agree strongly*.

	DS	D	N	A	AS
1. I frequently say to people, "I'm not sure."	5	4	3	2	1
2. I perform well in most situations in life.	1	2	3	4	5
3. I willingly offer advice to others.	1	2	3	4	5
4. Before making even a minor decision, I usually consult with several people.	5	4	3	2	1
5. I am generally willing to attempt new activities for which I have very little related skill or experience.	1	2	3	4	5
6. Speaking in front of the class or other group is (or was) a frightening experience for me.	5	4	3	2	1
7. I experience stress when people challenge me or put me on the spot.	5	4	3	2	1
8. I feel comfortable attending a social event by myself.	1	2	3	4	5
9. I'm much more of a winner than a loser.	1	2	3	4	5
1. I am cautious about making any substantial change in my life.	5	4	3	2	1
Total score: _____					

Scoring and Interpretation: Calculate your total score by adding the numbers circled. A tentative interpretation of the scoring is as follows:

45–50: Very high self-confidence with perhaps a tendency toward arrogance

38–44: A high, desirable level of self-confidence

30–37: Moderate, or average, self-confidence

10–29: Self-confidence needs strengthening

Strong Ethics. Ethics is a field of study in itself dealing with moral obligation, or separating right from wrong. The ethical person has values that result in treating others fairly. Values can be considered clear statements of what is critically important. Ethics become the vehicle for converting values into action. Having strong ethics contributes to humility because it is ethical to think and behave as if the opinions and rights of other people are important.

One question often asked in an ethical screen is "Is it right?" Assume that middle manager Bruce needs to promote somebody to the position of supervisor. The right thing to do would be to carefully evaluate the strengths of potential candidates, without quickly dismissing anyone as being too weak for the position. Asking, "Is it right?" leads to an act of humble leadership—acknowledging the strengths of others.

Another question in an ethical screen is "Who gets hurt?" The question is based on the notion of attempting to do the greatest good for the greatest number of people. Incorporating into one's ethical code the belief that other people should not be hurt leads to the humble action of not insulting or belittling others. Amanda, a logistics manager at a Ford Motor Company plant, is holding a virtual meeting with her team. Zeke, an inventory specialist, offers the suggestion that Ford should exit the automobile business and shift to other products because vehicle demand changes so rapidly.

Amanda's impulse is to insult Zeke by laughing at his suggestion. But instead, her ethical code of not hurting people propels Amanda to criticize Zeke's suggestion in a manner that reflects humility:

> *Zeke, I like the part of your suggestion that implies Ford should continue to diversify into fields other than vehicles. Yet top-management would probably be hesitant to exit a business we have been in for over 115 years. But I will investigate.*

Recognition of Own Limits. The attribute of recognizing one's own limits is part of self-awareness, and is included in many definitions of humility. When you recognize what you cannot do, or do well, it becomes necessary to ask others for help. Recognizing that you are wrong, or possibly might be wrong, facilitates expressing humility to others.

Mauro Da Silva, a software development specialist, writes that leaders are increasingly finding themselves without sufficient knowledge and information to arrive at an answer just because they are expected to. At this point, leaders need to be humbler and admit they do not know solutions to all the problems they are facing. With the recognition of their own limits, the leader will ask for help in a constructive manner.[4]

Anthony, the manager of an upscale restaurant, might say to the head chef,

> *I've got a big problem that maybe you can help me solve. Blake, our owner, tells me that we have to cut costs because our profits are shrinking. But the price of all our food and beverage supplies is increasing. I do not want to lay anyone off, and we don't dare cut the quality or size of our food. What do you see as a possibility for us to reduce costs?*

Motivation to Help Others. A fundamental attribute of humble leaders and professionals is that they are motivated to help other people. Psychology professor Joshua Hook says that "Humility is a very prosocial quality."[5] Prosocial motivation is the desire to exert effort to benefit others. Humility can help others for dozens of reasons including giving them the opportunity to express their opinion about work-related issues they perceive to be relevant.

The humble team leader with prosocial motivation can serve as a model for similar motivation among team members, and good performance might follow. Studies conducted with 191 teams in work settings and in the laboratory found prosocial motivation enhances cooperation within the group. In turn, the highest level of cooperation facilitates higher performance and being a good organizational citizen.[6] Prosocial motivation has a stronger effect when the work is more interdependent. A logical explanation is that when people depend on each other to accomplish a task, the willingness to help each other is more important.

The prosocial motivation of humble leaders is also important because it leads naturally to prosocial values while making decisions. Prosocial values, as with prosocial motivation, are aimed at helping people, such as explaining to team members how their work contributes to the good of the organization.

Mindfulness. As we mentioned briefly in the introduction to this chapter, mindfulness is a characteristic of a humble leader. Mindfulness is about being totally aware of the present and blocking out the past and future. A study conducted in Germany found that having the disposition of mindfulness was related to humility in samples of both leaders and professional workers.[7] Mindfulness contributes to humility because if you pay close attention to another person while he or she is talking, you communicate respect and an appreciation of that individual.

Mindfulness also contributes to humility indirectly by helping a leader make a humorous comment. As a way of being mindful, a leader will often observe the tension that has built up in an interpersonal interaction and look for an absurdity to help relieve the tension.[8] The person who provides low-key humor often appears humble. Imagine a general manager is listening to a dispute between manufacturing and marketing over the pricing of a product. The manufacturing head says the product cannot be produced at the low cost demanded by marketing. At the same time, the marketing head says that the product cannot be sold if manufacturing does not lower the cost. To relieve the tension, the general manager says, "Good enough. We have an impasse Let's shut down the plant and open a frozen yogurt stand."

The display of humility in the anecdote just presented is subtle. Instead of imposing his will in the situation, the general manager has made a humorous comment that is likely to prompt the manufacturing and marketing heads to attain a reasonable compromise. By so doing, the general manager is sending the message, "You two are smart enough to figure a way out of this impasse."

Executive Presence. A useful element of being a persuasive leader or professional is to exude *executive presence*, the ability to give off a general sense of poise, self-confidence, decisiveness, and dignity.[9] Individuals who enter a physical or online meeting with a smile, and readily converse with others are thought to have executive presence. At one time executive presence was referred to as the "it" factor, a mysterious quality that makes a person noticed in a positive manner. Charisma might be used as a synonym for executive presence.

It may appear paradoxical that executive presence is an attribute of humble leaders and professionals. Yet a dose of humility does contribute to executive presence. Walking into a room and asking questions about other people, rather than talking about oneself, is an example of a humble gesture that contributes to executive presence. Mary Lee Gannon, a writer about career topics, says that you know you have a high executive presence when you have the humility to admit your mistakes and learn from them.[10]

Another subtle link between executive presence and humility is pride. A person with executive presence exudes pride in the accomplishments of the group as well as in being part of the group. Being proud is usually interpreted as humility rather than arrogance. Visualize Roxanne, the CFO at a telecommunications company, who has outstanding quarterly results to report. In her first dissemination of these results to the executive group, Roxanne says, "I am so proud of what the company accomplished last quarter. Despite some heavy new competition, our earnings per share increased 14 percent last quarter." Roxanne has expressed pride, but her emphasis on the accomplishments of others suggests humility.

Interactions with Others as Attributes

Our second category of attributes of humble leaders and professionals incorporates those that reflect direct interactions with others. For example, a leader with humility values being a good team player. The personality trait of high cooperation might generate a spirit of being a team player, but the attribute of being a good team player shows up in interaction with others.

Focus on the Common Good. A few years ago, the Georgia Municipal Association held its annual conference with the theme, "Cities United: Lead to Succeed." Dublin, Georgia Mayor Phil Best pointed out that all the mayors aimed for the success of their cities, and that they must actively lead their communities to make it happen. He emphasized that leading Georgia cities to success would require a significant dose of humility. Best emphasized that being a leader is not about winning at all costs. It is about finding solutions to the challenges the mayors face, solutions firmly rooted in the "common good." Pursuing the common good is what should drive the mayors forward.

Best said perceptively,

> *To work toward the "common good" we must be willing to listen and seek to understand others, admit when we are wrong, cultivate and engage the talents of others and cooperate to meet our collective goals. It requires leadership steeped in humility … We've been given the privilege of leadership. I encourage you to govern in a spirit of humility.*[11]

The four steps best suggested are necessary for working toward a common good and have a humility component. You have to listen to and seek to understand others. Admitting when you are wrong helps unite people. It is important to actively cultivate and engage the talents of others. Cooperation is a key component of meeting collective goals. Best said, "We can't work toward the common good unless we decide to get real, drop the pretense and bring humility to the table." He also advised the other mayors he and they have been given the privilege of leadership, and encouraged them to govern with a spirit of humility.[12]

We concur with Mayor Best. A major attribute of a humble leader is to work with others toward a common good. Humility facilitates working toward the common good because a leader with humility is perceived as focusing more on positive outcomes rather than on personal gain. We return to this theme in Chapter 7 about servant leadership.

Empathy. Humility requires empathy, or the ability to see things from another person's perspective. Fred Garcia, the executive director of a crisis management and executive leadership institute, says that humility is what makes empathy possible.[13] The leader with empathy either with deliberate effort or intuitively understands the perspectives of other stakeholders. Empathy is a vital component of humility because it indicates that the leader will at least give the other person's viewpoint a careful listen.

Empathy does not necessarily mean that you sympathize with the other person. For example, CEO Garth might carefully listen to and understand an employee group's demand that all workers should receive paid leave on their birthday. He communicates an understanding of this point of view, but he does not submit to the demand.

The empathy aspect of active listening and humility is recognized as a vital skill for a wide variety of workers. Geoff Colvin, an established business writer, observes that there is a mushrooming demand for employees with affective, nonlogical abilities that cut across the economy. Empathy, viewed as sensing at a deep level the feelings and thoughts of others, is the foundation. In this regard, a retailing CEO from Germany said his biggest hiring challenge is to find people who are empathetic and collaborative.[14] Some of the leadership success of Microsoft CEO Satya Nadella is attributed to his ability to empathize with employees and customers. Nadella believes that it is his mission to teach, listen, and absorb new ideas rather than thinking he has all the answers.[15] As with other effective leaders and managers, Nadella uses listening to show humility and help build relationships with people.

Kindness and Approachability. A basic attribute of a humble leader is the expression of kindness. Research suggests that group members enjoy working for a leader who takes charge but creates and implements rules in a kind, thoughtful manner. *Kindness* from a leader has many different interpretations yet behaviors typically thought to be kind include showing a genuine interest in the work activities carried out by group members, their careers, and personal lives.

Kindness on the part of a leader can create an enjoyable work environment, as well as more loyal and committed employees. An underlying reason is that the human brain is wired to respond well to kindness and respect. Former organizational anthropologist and executive coach, Judith Glaser observes, "When someone is kind and respectful to us, our brains produce more oxytocin and dopamine, which helps us relax, feel open to others, and be more sharing and cooperative."[16] Being open and welcoming to collaboration is beneficial to the teamwork required in most workplaces.

A dimension of leadership related to kindness is *consideration*, the degree to which the leader creates an environment of emotional support, warmth, friendliness, and trust. (By dimension, we mean that the attribute has been measured by questionnaires in many studies.) The leader creates this environment by being friendly and approachable, and looking out for the welfare of the group. A considerate leader also keeps the group abreast of new developments, and does small favors for the group. Two small favors that often meet with high acceptance are getting group or team T-shirts, or organizing a family picnic for the group.

Leaders who score high on the consideration dimension typically are friendly and trustworthy, earn respect, and have a warm relationship with group members. Leaders with low scores on consideration typically are authoritarian and impersonal in their relationships with group members. Three questionnaire items measuring the consideration factor are as follows:

1. Do personal favors for people in the work group.
2. Treat all people in the work group as your equal.
3. Do little things to make it pleasant to be a staff member.[17]

Approachability results from a person being kind: if you are kind, you are approachable. Being humble also makes you approachable because most people feel comfortable interacting with a person who has a reasonable degree of humility. One reason is that if you are perceived as humble, most people would sense that you would be willing to discuss a point of view different from yours without getting upset.

Visibility and Social Presence. An effective way of making an impact as a leader is to be visible to group members, thereby maintaining the perception of being present. There is a strong temptation for leaders to stay in their own work area performing analytical work or dealing with email. Being visible allows for spontaneous communication with group members, and a relaxed atmosphere in which to hear about problems. Humble leaders take naturally to being visible because they enjoy interacting with and listening to group members.

Giving Emotional Support and Encouragement. One aspect of consideration deserves a separate mention. Supportive behavior toward team members usually increases leadership effectiveness. A supportive leader gives frequent encouragement and praise and also displays caring and kindness even about nonwork-related matters such as the health of a worker's ill family member.

Keep in mind that encouragement means to fill with courage. One of the many work-related ways of encouraging people is to ask for their input about important decisions. Emotional support generally improves morale and sometimes improves productivity. In the long term, emotional support and encouragement may bolster a person's self-esteem. Being emotionally supportive comes naturally to a leader who is empathetic and warm.

Giving encouragement was also the eighth leadership principle of Dale Carnegie, the famous early proponent of human relations principles in work and personal life. In later years, Tessa E. Basford and Andrea Molberg searched for empirical evidence for the validity of Carnegie's leadership principles, including encouragement. Overall, they found support for Carnegie's recommendations to use encouragement. Encouragement is linked to improvement of job performance and attitudes, probably because encouragement boosts feelings of self-worth.[18]

An indirect, but effective, way of giving emotional support to group members is to make them happy by creating conditions that foster happiness. Psychology professor Sonja Lyubomirsky has found that employees are happier when they are helping others. Based on a study at Coca Cola in Madrid, she found that acts of kindness make employees feel more connected to each other and their jobs. Furthermore, co-workers observed what was happening, and were inspired to replicate kindness in such ways as complimenting each other and bringing coffee.[19] The leader's role here would be to encourage employees to be kind to each other.

Authenticity and Honesty. Authenticity is about being genuine and honest about your personality, values, and beliefs as well as having integrity. Bill George, a Harvard Business School professor and former chairman and CEO of Medtronic, developed the concept of authentic leadership. In his words, "Authentic leaders demonstrate a passion for their purpose, practice their values consistently, and lead with their hearts as well as their heads. They establish long-term meaningful relationships and have the self-discipline to get results. They know who they are."[20]

George has explained more recently that people who follow their leadership compass toward *true north* can achieve authentic leadership. True north refers to a person's most deeply held beliefs, his or her values, and the principles that lead the person.[21] Being passionate about your purpose and being unwavering in your values helps make you a humble rather than a self-centered leader.

To become an authentic leader and to demonstrate authenticity, be yourself rather than attempting to be a replica of someone else. Others respond to your leadership, partly because you are genuine rather than phony. The authentic leader can emphasize different values and characteristics to different people without being phony. For example, a corporate-level manager at Goodyear service centers might engage in more banter when he or she visits a service center than when meeting with financial analysts.

Willingness to Be a Team Player. A leader who is a good team player displays humility. The leader demonstrates that he or she does not feel beyond carrying out some of the activities that constitute the work of the group. Interacting extensively with team members serves as a model of teamwork because it illustrates the mechanism by which team development takes place—frequent informal communication. While interacting with team members, the leader can emphasize that he or she is a team member and therefore humble. For example, it is better to say "We have to get this done by Thursday," than "You have to get this done by Thursday." The accompanying self-quiz provides you with an opportunity to think about your willingness to be a team player.

Considering that being a team player is a key attribute of a humble leader, the following are a handful of practical suggestions as to how a team leader can be an effective team player:

- Share power with group members because a good team player avoids hogging power and making all the decisions. As each team member takes the opportunity to exert power, he or she feels more like a major contributor to team effort—a result that suits the humble leader.
- Power sharing can also take the form of team members feeling free to offer constructive criticism, and providing feedback to the team leader as to how well his or her suggestions are working.
- Sharing credit for good deeds with team members. Instead of focusing on yourself as the person responsible for a work achievement, point out that the achievement was a group effort. (This attribute is widely practiced in business and sports, and has attained cliché status.) You will make a poor team player if you try to grab all the glory for ideas that work and distance yourself from ideas that do not work. A humble team leader wants all team members to succeed. You will appear by praising the people you work with rather than hogging any praise for the team.
- Display a helpful, cooperative attitude. Working cooperatively with team members is virtually synonymous with team play and displays humility at the same time. Suppose a team member has what she thinks is a creative idea for improving a business process, but she believes that the idea needs more work. Listening to her and adding relevant input would be a robust example of displaying a helpful, cooperative attitude.
- Share information and opinions with team members. Teamwork is facilitated when the team leader shares information and opinions with team members. Sharing information is likely to be perceived as an act of humility because the leader does not feel that he or she should be guarding information in order to stay in control. Another important aspect of sharing information is to provide technical expertise or knowledge of the task. Although this is an obvious part of a leader's role, a humble leader is more likely to understand its importance.

- Follow the Golden Rule. The ancient adage, "Treat others the way you would want them to treat you" provides a firm foundation for the leader to be a good team player. Although some people may dismiss the Golden Rule as a syrupy platitude, it still works. For example, you would probably want your manager to cover for you if you faced a sudden family problem, so you would do the same for a team member.
- Avoid actions that could sabotage or undermine the group in any way. Frequently criticizing the team directly or complaining about them to management or other outsiders works against the best interest of the group. Team members will most likely hear that you criticized them to an outsider, thus doing damage to your ability to work cooperatively with them and be perceived as a team player.

To think more about your tendencies toward being a team player, you are invited to take the accompanying self-quiz.

TEAM PLAYER ATTITUDES

Directions: Describe how well you agree with each of the following statements, using the following scale: *Disagree Strongly* (DS); *Disagree* (D); *Neutral* (N); *Agree* (A); *Agree Strongly* (AS). Circle the number in the appropriate column.

	DS	D	N	A	AS
1. I am at my best when working alone.	5	4	3	2	1
2. I have belonged to clubs and teams ever since I was a child.	1	2	3	4	5
3. It takes far too long to get work accomplished with a group.	5	4	3	2	1
4. I like the friendship of working in a group.	1	2	3	4	5
5. I would prefer to run a one-person business than to be a member of a large firm.	5	4	3	2	1
6. It's difficult to trust others in the group on key assignments.	5	4	3	2	1
7. Encouraging others comes to me naturally.	1	2	3	4	5
8. I like the give-and-take of ideas that is possible in a group.	1	2	3	4	5
9. It is fun for me to share responsibility with other group members.	1	2	3	4	5

	DS	D	N	A	AS
10. Much more can be accomplished by a team than by the same number of people working alone.	1	2	3	4	5
Total Score _____					

Scoring and Interpretation: Add the numbers you circled to obtain your total score.

41–50: You have strong positive attitudes toward being a team member and working cooperatively with other members.

30–40: You have moderately favorable attitudes toward being a team member and working cooperatively with other members.

10–29: You prefer working by yourself to being a team member. To work effectively in a company that emphasizes teamwork, you may need to develop more positive attitudes toward working jointly with others.

A LEADER WITH HUMILITY: RAJ GUPTA, FORMER CEO OF ROHM AND HAAS

Raj Gupta was the CEO of chemical company Rohm and Haas for ten prosperous years. During his 40 years with the company, Gupta worked in many parts of the world and held many leadership and professional positions. As he reflected on his life in an interview with Michael Useem of the Wharton School, he talked about the lessons he learned from his father: "Graft was pervasive in India, but my father never accepted one rupee of bribe in his life." Another lesson he learned was to respect everyone, whether they were higher-ups or the servers, cleaners, or drivers. Everyone should be treated with respect.

Gupta was also influenced by several executives he worked with early in his career. From a man named Larry Wilson, he learned the importance of maintaining your composure and calm demeanor under stress. Gupta also learned how to be a good listener and to always present yourself as the person in charge.

During the time when Rohm and Haas was acquiring three companies in rapid succession, Gupta approached the task with an element of humility. He said,

It was a bigger task than I had thought for sure. The way I approached this was, number one, to make sure that I got to hear from the board, each of the board members, and met with them individually to understand what they liked about the way we worked and what we could improve on. I made sure they knew me and they felt I had access to them and they had access to me.

During his career, Gupta served on the board of several major companies, and worked with many business leaders. He believes that to be an effective board member a person needs learning agility and skills. It is also important for business leaders to surround themselves with people smarter than them, and sometimes get out of their way as well. Gupta also talked about the importance of leaders learning to balance a healthy ego with humility. He thinks that humility opens you to a lot of good input from outside. If you are approachable and humble, people with tell you what they like about you, and what they do not like.

Gupta believes that having self-confidence and a healthy ego is an important part of demonstrating your confidence and self-belief. You have to have a healthy ego. In Gupta's words, "On the other hand, if you are humble and available for a conversation and open feedback, it makes you a better person and a better leader."[22]

As you have most likely observed, Gupta's thoughts reflect many of the attributes of humble leaders.

GUIDELINES FOR ACTION

1. Studying the attributes of humble leaders and professionals is a worthwhile activity because they can often be learned and developed.
2. Focusing enthusiasm and optimism on the accomplishments of others is a relatively easy way to implement humility and build cordial relationships.
3. A major contributor to facilitating lifetime learning is to develop a *growth mindset*, or believing that it is possible to develop your talents through hard work, good strategies, and input from others. A growth mindset gives you a humble view of your intelligence.
4. Being humble does not mean that you lower your self-confidence. Instead, it is usually best to be in the middle of the continuum between self-confidence and arrogance.

5. Having strong ethics contributes to humility because it is ethical to think and behave as if the opinions and rights of other people are important.

6. A fundamental attribute of humble leaders and professionals is that have prosocial motivation, or the desire to help others. Searching for ways to help others therefore enhances your effectiveness.

7. Mindfulness contributes to humility because if you pay close attention to another person while he or she is talking, you communicate respect and appreciation for that individual.

8. Walking into a room and asking questions about other people, rather than talking about oneself is a humble gesture that contributes to executive presence. It might be possible to implement the same tactic in a virtual meeting.

9. Pursuing the common good is a robust act of humility, so it is worthwhile identifying what the common good might be in a given group situation.

10. Displaying empathy is another major attribute of humility. Make a deliberate effort to understand the perspectives of other stakeholders.

11. A field-tested way of creating being considerate is to be friendly and approachable, or through small gestures, such as doing small favors for people.

12. A leader who is a good team player displays humility, such as demonstrating that he or she does not feel beyond carrying out some of the activities that constitute the work of the group. Two other notable approaches are to share power with team members, and share credit for group accomplishments with the group.

NOTES

1. "Humble Leadership: What Is it?" https://humaninterest.co.za, 2020.
2. Carol Dweck, "What having a 'Growth Mindset' Actually Means," *Harvard Business Review* (https://hbr.org), January 13, 2016, pp. 1–3.
3. Christopher Nelson, "Leadership with a Touch of Humility," *The Imaginative Conservative* (www.theimaginativeconservative.org), February 26, 2015, p. 2.
4. Mauro Da Silva, "Humble Leadership," *The Learning Apprentice* (www.learningapprentice.com), August 29, 2018, p. 1.

5. Cited in Patty Onderko, "Do These 6 Things to Be More Humble," *Success* (www .success.com), December 2015, p. 1.
6. Jia Hu and Robert C. Liden, "Making a Difference in the Teamwork: Linking Team Prosocial Motivation in Team Processes and Effectiveness," *Academy of Management Journal*, August 2015, pp. 1102–1137.
7. Armin Pircher Verdorfer, "Examining Mindfulness and Its Relation to Humility, Motivation to Lead, and Actual Servant Leadership Behaviors," https://link .springer.com, Volume 7, August 2016, pp. 950–961.
8. Bob Emrich, "The One Leadership Tool Entrepreneurs Don't use Enough," *Chicago Tribune Business*, November 8, 2015, p. 6.
9. "What is Executive Presence? Definition and Examples," *https://study.com*, 2020, p. 1.
10. Mary Lee Gannon, "How to Know if You Have Executive Presence," *Ladders* (www .theladders.com), October 3, 2018, p. 2.
11. Phil Best, "Transformative Leadership is Humble Servant Leadership," *Georgia's Cities Magazine* (www.gacities.com), August 14, 2019, pp. 1–2.
12. "Dublin Mayor Phil Best Elected President of GMA," *Georgia Municipal Association* (www.gacities.com), June 24, 2019, pp. 2–3.
13. Fred Garcia, "Humility as an Attribute of Effective leadership," www.compro.biz, July 23, 2018, p. 32.
14. Geoff Colvin, "Employers are Looking for New Hires with Something Extra, Empathy," *Fortune*, September 27, 2014, p. 55.
15. Harry McCraken, "Satya Nadella Rewrites Microsoft's Code," *Fast Company*, September 8, 2017, pp. 52–53.
16. Cited in Leah Thomas, "1 Super Rare Sign You're Supposed to be a Leader, According to Research," *Leah Thomas Via Fairygodboss* (www.fairygodboss.com), November 1, 2018, pp. 1–2 The preceding discussion is also based on Thomas.
17. The original research on consideration stems from Ralph M. Stogdill and Alvin E. Coons, eds., *Leader Behavior: Its Description and Measurement* (Columbus, Ohio: The Ohio State University Bureau of Business Research, 1957).
18. Tessa E. Basford and Andrea Molberg, "Dale Carnegie's Leadership Principles: Examining the Theoretical and Empirical Support," *Journal of Leadership Studies*, no 4, 2013, pp. 37–38.
19. Cited in interview by Arianne Cohen, "What I Wear to Work: Sonja Lyubomirsky," *Bloomberg Businessweek*, January 12–January 18, 2015, p. 71.
20. Bill George, Peter Sims, Andrew N. McLean, and Diana Mayer, "Discovering Your Authentic Leadership," *Harvard Business Review*, February 2007, p. 130.
21. Interview of Bill George by James Tehrani, "'Northern Exposure' to Leadership," *Workforce*, September 2015, p. 12.
22. "Why Leaders Must Balance Ego with Humility," *Knowledge@Wharton* (www .knowledge.wharton.upenn.edu), June 30, 2017, pp. 1–15; Raj Gupta, "How I did It: Rohm and Haas's Former CEO on Pulling Off a Sweet Deal in a Down Market," *Harvard Business Review*, November 2010.

5

Interpersonal Aspects of Humble Leadership

The major components of leadership involve interaction with people so it follows that leadership humility has considerable interpersonal aspects. We refer to "major components" because all of leadership does not involve direct interaction with people. Leaders also spend time in creative problem-solving and strategy formulation, often by consulting others but sometimes via independent thought.

Our focus in this chapter is on those aspects of humble leadership dealing most directly with building and sustaining interpersonal relationships. Assume that the vice president of finance, Madison, is a humble leader who as part of her humility freely expresses gratitude when deserved. By expressing gratitude to a group member for a job well done, as well as for willingly accepting any assignment, Madison helps build constructive relationships with work associates. A frequently observed reality in leadership and human resource management is that the vast majority of workers do not receive as much gratitude as they would like from their superiors and co-workers.

BUILDING CONNECTIONS WITH OTHERS

As observed by Beth Coleman, an instructor at the FBI Academy, humility is proving to be one of the most critical behaviors that leaders need to develop and communicate to establish connectivity with their teams. With connectivity, the team is likely to experience the benefits of

DOI: 10.4324/9781003461784-5

improved morale, stronger trust, and increased productivity. All of these results would be perceived as desirable by most leaders. Some evidence has accumulated that people will follow a leader regardless of rank or position with whom they feel a connection. In contrast, they are less likely to follow a leader who they perceive as disconnected, arrogant, and out of touch with them.[1]

To make effective use of the concept of *connections with others*, you need to pin down some of the behaviors associated with making connections. Today "being connected" often refers to any digital contact with another person or product, such as being 1 of 3 million Twitter followers of a celebrity or politician. Here are some of the behaviors and attitudes included in building connections with others in a work setting:[2]

- Open-mindedness, open communication, and being in touch with others;
- Positive interactions with others such as complimenting actions that please the leader;
- Helping group members understand the purpose of the organization as well as the purpose of their work;
- Displaying strong ethics and fairness in dealing with employees;
- Accepting or sharing blame when the group effort fails, such as not getting a prototype delivered on time;
- Delegating decision-making to group members when appropriate;
- Communicating a mission or vision that employees understand, accept, and perceive as unifying, such as the vision of Lexus: "The relentless pursuit of perfection";
- Encouraging employee voice (a say) about how well the team is doing.

The statements in the above bulleted list are helpful in understanding attitudes and behaviors that contribute to making connections with group members. Here are a few sentences of dialogue between marketing manager Craig and customer-care manager Alicia that illustrate connectivity:

Craig: How are you holding up these days Alicia? I've heard that hundreds of our customers are complaining that the upgrades we made to our satellite dishes work poorly on cloudy days.

Alicia: Thanks for recognizing the problem. My team has been overwhelmed dealing with complaints. We don't have an answer yet as to how soon the company can fix the problem.

Craig: Hang in there Alicia. You and your team always come through during peaks in customer concerns. We are working with our engineering group to give you the help you and your team need and deserve.

Observe that Craig is connecting with Alicia by both expressing empathy for her work challenges, and also showing support to help him resolve the problem.

PERSONAL RELATIONSHIPS

Esteemed organizational psychologist Edgar A. Schein and his son Peter A. Schein, a Silicon Valley innovator, argue that as organizations face more complex, interdependent tasks, leadership must become more personal. A personal relationship overcomes the professional distance between the leader and a subordinate or a professional and the client. The personal aspect helps build open, trusting communication that makes more collaborative problem-solving and innovation possible. Humble leadership is well suited to building personal relationships because subordinates feel appreciated and understood.

As observed by Schein and Schein, managers, direct reports, team members, and people from outside the team are making a point to get to know each other on a more personal level. The result of building these personal relationships is more openness in communication, more trust, and the psychological safety to speak up knowing that the person will not be criticized for submitting a weak idea.

As proposed by Schein and Schein, a Level 2 relationship is personal, cooperative, and trusting as found in friendships and effective teams. In a Level 2 relationship, the leader or professional conveys "I see you." This does not necessarily mean "I like you," or "I want to be your friend," or "Let's get our families together." Instead, it means through my words, demeanor, and body language that I am aware of your presence, and that in this relationship we are working together and are interdependent. We are also trying to trust each other. We should try to see each other as more than a work associate, but as a whole person. In this sense, work relationships should be like personal relationships in which people often see each other as whole persons.

A Level 2 relationship also allows for the power-sharing typical of humble leaders. Within the work group, anyone who has pertinent information and expertise is encouraged to speak up and improve whatever task the group is attempting to accomplish.[3]

GRATITUDE AS A FORM OF HUMILITY

According to motivation scientist Heidi Grant, an important purpose of gratitude is to strengthen our relationships with people we rely on. To express gratitude is to make a deliberate point of being thankful for the positive things in your life. Gratitude functions like a glue that binds you and your benefactor together, enabling you to tap the same well repeatedly knowing that your support will not run dry. Executives often attribute success to their own efforts rather than expressing appreciation for the organizational resources that support their achievements. Expressing gratitude, however, is a behavior that comes easily to humble leaders and professionals. Yet not all approaches to expressing gratitude are equally effective in relationship building.

When we express gratitude to others, we have a tendency to talk about ourselves when we should be thinking about the other person. When we receive help and support the tendency of most people is to talk about how the favor or assistance made *them* feel. For example, "I felt so relieved," or "I was able to cope better with my workload." The research of Grant and others suggests that expressing gratitude should not be all about you. The people who helped you want to see themselves positively and to feel understood and cared for. This is difficult for them to do if you talk only about yourself.

The more effective type of gratitude is to use "other praising" rather than focusing on the self-benefit. Acknowledge and validate your benefactor's actions, in such ways as "You go out of your way to help during crunch time" or "You're really good at setting up the agenda for the meeting." Doing so will strengthen your relationship with the other person and will enhance the effectiveness of your humility.[4]

Additional examples of other praising include:

- "What you did to get your data analysis done in such a short period of time shows how responsible you are."
- "You go out of your way to make sure our construction estimates are close to the final price."
- "My opinion is that you are really good at finding us new clients."

Examples of self-benefit include:

- "You getting the data analysis done on time helped me relax a little about the project."
- "Your accurate construction estimates make me look much smarter as the construction manager."
- "Your ability to find new clients makes it much easier for me to reach our quarterly goals."

A related approach for the humble leader to use as an expression of gratitude is informal recognition. (Recognizing the strengths of others is a key component of humility.) Praising workers for good performance is a major type of informal recognition. An effective form of praise describes the worker's performance rather than merely making an evaluation. Describing good performance might take this form: "You turned an angry customer into an ally who has referred new business to us." A straightforward evaluation would be, "You did a great job with that angry customer." Even more effective would be to combine the two statements.

Generic praise, such as telling all workers on the team they are doing a great job can be discouraging, because the team members will not feel they are being recognized as individuals. A useful principle of effective praise is that it should be true, sincere, deserved and meaningful. Here is an example of praising good performance:

Derek, you made an amazing presentation this morning. I especially liked the slides you used to illustrate the pricing strategies we are facing. That really helped me make sense of a complex issue. Thanks for the hard work you put into the presentation.

Jana Gallus, an assistant professor of strategy and behavioral decision-making at the UCLA Anderson School of Management, recommends that managers use *discretionary* rewards to informally recognize good performance. Discretionary rewards refer to honors where a manager, under no obligation, chooses to recognize noteworthy behavior that goes beyond what is expected and that isn't already acknowledged by other rewards. For example, a high level of collaboration can be recognized with teamwork honors. The element of surprise increases the potency of the award for the winners.[5]

Although praise costs no money and only requires a few moments of time, many workers feel they do not receive enough praise. Leaders therefore have a good opportunity to increase motivation by the simple act of praising good deeds. Other informal approaches to recognizing good performance and expressing gratitude include taking an employee to lunch, a fist bump from the manager or team leader, and putting flowers on an employee's desk. Email and text messages are other handy tools for giving praise and recognition. Because gratitude and praise are such a key part of a humble leader's tool kit, the accompanying table about saying "well done" is presented here.

HELPING OTHERS GROW

As Bradley P. Owens and David K. Heckman concluded in their pioneering study of humility and leadership, humble leadership can lead to employees who constantly keep growing and improving. Although the 55 leaders interviewed were from totally different organizations, they all agreed that the essence of leader humility involves being a model for followers of how to grow. The humble leaders in the study were described as "models of learning."[6]

Leaders with humility displayed openness to new ideas and information, listened before speaking, and were highly receptive to feedback. Humble leaders would also be models of personal growth and learning by initiating role reversals with group members. This meant that the leaders would assume the group member role and place the group member in the leader/trainer role.

TWENTY WAYS TO SAY "WELL DONE"

The various ways of expressing thanks for a job well done listed below focus mostly on other praising but also include a few self-benefit statements.

1. I'm proud you are on my team.	11. I have great confidence in your talent.
2. Congratulations on a terrific job.	12. You've grasped the concept well.
3. You're so helpful. Thank you.	13. Your customer service skills are sensational.
4. You really made a difference with your suggestion.	14. Your sales skills are sensational.
5. Thanks so much for your considerate effort.	15. You are a valuable team member.
6. I really admire your perseverance.	16. Your efforts make a big difference.
7. You've made my day by solving this problem.	17. You are hitting high productivity.
8. You're a champion.	18. Our customers love you.
9. Wow, what an amazing accomplishment.	19. You have made it possible for us to attain our goals.
10. Great accomplishment. You made all of us look good.	20. Your work ethic is a model for the team.

Rather than only telling followers how to do things, humble leaders were described as showing group members how to perform a task, and then seeking feedback from the learners. For example, a leader might say, "Hey, let's learn this together. Let's make some sales calls together. Maybe you can see me making a call and can give me some pointers in what I do right, and what I do wrong. Then you can try it."

It seemed that no group member task was too menial for leaders with humility. They would serve as a model for a wide variety of follower tasks from sales calls, to custodial work, to basic labor. In one extreme example, a high-ranking military leader broke his leg helping lift a large generator off a truck with his soldiers. The officer's only lament was that he would not be able to run with his soldiers in the immediate future.

By being a model of eagerness to learn, the humble leaders appeared to be intent on fostering a positive, proactive attitude about acquiring new knowledge. At the same time, the same leaders gained a deeper understanding of how to best help group members overcome challenges. Humble leaders did not only talk about the importance of continual learning, or supporting training programs for learning and development. They also provided an example of how to develop by being honest about areas for improvement including acknowledging mistakes and limitations.

An attitude of humble leaders that catalyzed an interest in growth was to tell group members that it is okay to be a "work in progress" here. The leaders emphasized that mistakes in acquiring new skills are almost inevitable, and are therefore tolerated. Followers were influenced to believe that apprehension was natural and acceptable when acquiring new knowledge. A leader might say, "I can see what a whale of a challenge it is to learn how to incorporate artificial intelligence into your analysis. Take the time you need to learn how to apply AI to our problems."

Coaching with Humility

As implied in the above discussion of helping others grow, humble leadership includes coaching. Coaching is the natural vehicle for leaders and professionals to improve performance and behavior of their subordinates and clients. For example, a finance specialist might coach her boss, the manager of a distribution center, on how to minimize recurring cash flow problems. Humility is involved in coaching because the focus is on the person being coached, not on the accomplishments of the person doing the coaching. Here we look at suggestions for coaching with humility. The suggestions are a mix of coaching to improve substandard performance and coaching to enhance the performance of a group member already performing acceptably or well.

1. *Focus Feedback on What Is Wrong with the Work and Behavior Rather than the Employee's Attitude and Personality.* When the feedback attacks a person's self-image, he or she is likely to become hostile. A defensive person is more likely to focus on getting even rather than getting better. Another way to upset the person being coached is to exaggerate the nature of the poor performance, such as saying, "You've committed the same mistake 100 times," when you have only observed the mistake four times. Keep in mind that it would be acting out of character for a humble leader to attack another person's self-image.

2. *Build Relationships.* Effective coaches build relationships with group members, and at the same time coaching is a way of building effective relationships. Having established rapport with group members facilitates entering into a coaching relationship with them. One of the reasons that leaders who display humility are effective coaches is that their approach to leadership focuses on relationship building.

3. *Give on-the-Spot Positive Feedback as Warranted.* A synthesis of information about effective feedback suggests that performance is most likely to improve when team members are told what is working.[7] Assume that a marketing analyst is being coached by her manager about providing more depth to her reports about the appeal of certain products. When the manager receives a report that contains the depth he is seeking, the manager sends a text message to the analyst saying, "Nice work on the anti-aging food supplement report. Just the depth I need." Providing positive feedback comes naturally to a person who leads with humility.

4. *Be Timely with Negative Feedback.* Negative feedback should be given close in time to the incident of poor performance. If you observe a worker being rude to a customer, do not wait until the annual performance evaluation to share your observation. Schedule a coaching session as soon as feasible. The worker might be rude to many more customers until he or she receives your criticism. Offering negative feedback in a thoughtful, constructive way is an act of humility.

5. *Give Emotional Support.* By being helpful and constructive, the leader provides much-needed emotional support to the group member who is not performing at his or her best. A coaching session should not be an interrogation. An effective way of giving emotional support is to use positive rather than negative motivators. For example, the leader might say, "I like some of the things you accomplished yesterday, and I have a few suggestions that might bring you closer to performing at your best."

6. *Listen Actively and Empathize.* An essential component of coaching employees requires careful listening to both their presentation of facts and feelings. Your listening will encourage the employee to talk. As the employee talks about his or her problem, you may develop a better understanding of how to improve performance. As you listen actively, the opportunity to show empathy will arise naturally. Suppose the employee blames being behind schedule on the servers being down so frequently. You might show empathy by saying, "Yes,

I know it is frustrating to have a computer crash when faced with a deadline. Yet we all have to deal with this problem." Empathy, of course, is a key attribute of the humble leader.

7. *Ask Good Questions.* An effective workplace coach asks questions that help people understand their needs for improvement. Start the coaching session by asking a question, thereby encouraging the person being coached to be an active participant immediately. Consultant Marilyn J. Darling says that effective coaching is based on asking good questions. She notes that the simpler the question, the better, (Notice that the questions are open-ended, therefore encouraging conversation.)

    • What are you trying to accomplish?
    • How will you know if you have succeeded?
    • What obstacles do you believe are stopping you?
    • How can I help you succeed?[8]

8. *Engage in Joint Problem-Solving.* Work together to resolve the performance problem. One *reason* joint problem-solving is effective is that it conveys a helpful and constructive attitude on the part of the leader. Another is that the employee often needs the superior's assistance in overcoming work problems. The leader is in a better position to address certain problems than the employee. Joint problem-solving comes naturally to humble leaders because they do not think they have all the answers.

9. *Offer Constructive Advice.* Constructive advice can be useful to the employee with performance problems. A recommended way of giving advice is first to ask an insightful question. You might ask the employee, "Could the real cause of your problem be poor work habits?" If the employee agrees, you can then offer some specific advice about improving work habits. As part of giving advice, it is more effective to suggest a person do something rather than try to do something. For example, it is more persuasive to say, "Be at our staff meetings on time," than to say, "Try to be at our staff meetings on time." "Trying" something gives a person an excuse not to succeed.

    An especially effective aspect of constructive advice is to help the person who is performing poorly understand the link between the negative act and attaining key goals, such as increased revenue and productivity.[8] Suppose a store manager typically neglects to respond to questions asked by customers using the "Contact Us" function. His or her leader/

coach might point out, "Customers who are ignored will soon ignore us, leading to the loss of some important customers, along with some important sales. We need every customer we can get or keep."

10. *Give the Poor Performer an Opportunity to Observe and Model Someone Who Exhibits Acceptable Performance.* A simple example of modeling would be for the manager to show the employee how to operate a piece of equipment properly. A more complex example of modeling would be to have the poor performer observe an effective employee making a sale or conducting a job interview. In each case, the ineffective performer should be given opportunities to repeat the activity. As described in the previous section, humble leaders often serve as a model of learning for a group member. The leader might therefore sometimes serve as a model to emulate.

11. *Obtain a Commitment to Change.* Ineffective performers frequently agree to make improvements but are not really committed to change. At the end of a session, discuss the employee's true interest in changing. One clue that commitment may be lacking is when the employee too readily accepts everything you say about the need for change. Another clue is agreement about the need for change but with no display of emotion. In either case, further discussion is warranted. The humble leader would find it natural to listen carefully to detect if there is a real commitment to change.

12. *When Feasible, Conduct Some Coaching Sessions Outside of the Performance Evaluation.* The coaching experience should focus on development and improvement, whereas the performance review is likely to be perceived by the ineffective performer as a time for judging his or her performance. Despite this perception, performance evaluations should include an aspect of development. The humble leader enjoys interacting regularly with group members, and would therefore enjoy coaching outside the formality of a performance review.

13. *Applaud Good Results.* Effective coaches on the playing field and in the workplace are cheerleaders. They give encouragement and positive reinforcement by applauding good results. Some effective coaches shout in joy when a poor performer achieves standard performance; others clap their hands in applause.

The below checklist provides more insight into the attributes of an effective coach.

ATTRIBUTES OF AN EFFECTIVE COACH

Below is a list of attributes of effective coaches. Place a checkmark next to each attribute that you need to develop along those lines (for example, whether you need to become more patient). On a separate document, design an action plan for improvement for each attribute that you need to develop. An action plan for improving patience might be, "I'll ask for feedback from people I know well to tell me when I appear too impatient. I will also try to develop self-control about my impatience."

Attribute (Trait, Attitude, or Behavior)

1. Empathy ☐

2. Listen with care ☐

3. Good intuition into people ☐

4. Patient with people ☐

5. Smile easily when I agree with somebody ☐

6. Care about the welfare of people ☐

7. Will listen to criticism of my suggestions ☐

8. Enjoy helping other people ☐

9. Feel confident that I can help people ☐

10. Prefer to collaborate than compete with group members ☐

11. Makes my day when I help someone ☐

12. Enthusiasm for working with people ☐

13. Believe most people can attain new heights ☐

14. Have high expectations for group members ☐

15. As a coach, I believe that others can outperform me ☐

16. Can give honest feedback ☐

17. Focus on telling the truth ☐

18. Usually warm and friendly ☐

19. Enjoy helping others perform better than me ☐

20. Develop trust and respect for others ☐

Reverse Mentoring and Humility

Another effective way a humble leader can build effective relationships within the group is through *reverse mentoring*, or being taught something specific from a younger group member. The typical scenario is for the younger group member to coach the leader about computer technology. Yet younger people have valuable skills and knowledge in many areas in addition to computer technology. Among the dozens of possibilities would be knowledge about a second language, the cultural values of a particular group, packaging design, fashion design, and mathematics.

Humble leaders take naturally to building relationships through reverse mentoring because one of their fundamental beliefs is that they do not have all the knowledge to perform their work in an outstanding manner. Retired Four-Star General Stanley McChrystal was a strong believer in practicing reverse mentoring. The Army's tactics and equipment changed dramatically between the time McChrystal joined the Army and his promotion to four-star general. During his later years in command, McChrystal recognized that his decades of experience were not directly relevant to the younger soldiers. With humility, he wondered if she should still be in charge.

McChrystal recognized that he had to be honest with himself and his troops. He admitted he had some knowledge gaps and asked his direct reports to teach him. In return, McChrystal, promised to provide them with wisdom based on his lengthy experience. Rather than questioning his capability and legitimacy as a leader, the troops gave McChrystal credit for admitting where he needed fresh knowledge. The entire battalion benefited from the exchange of knowledge.[9]

Macro-Managing Subordinates

Leaders with humility take naturally to avoiding micromanagement because they usually assume that the person performing a task has more job-relevant knowledge than they do. As noted by management consultant Jeff Kirschner, the ability to step away from micromanagement and trust the team is a good demonstration of humility. When a CEO demonstrates humility, he or she builds trust and fosters followership for executives. They are provided with the bandwidth to carry out their roles with more freedom.[10]

Leaders who are deficient in humility tend to be micromanagers. They are so focused on ensuring everything is done their way that they lose sight of the group goal. Humble leaders are aware that micromanagement can backfire, so they work hard to promote group member autonomy. Humble leaders are comfortable in backing off and practicing *macro-management* because they accept the reality that they are not always the person with the best answer to an individual or group problem. Equally important, humble leaders are confident in their employees' skills and knowledge, and are open to new ideas.[11]

As a macro-manager, the humble leader takes a hands-off approach to leading employees, and allows group members to perform their tasks without much supervision. A potential pitfall of macro-management is that many employees want and need close supervision and feedback, particularly when they are acquiring new skills. Take the example of a woman who has a key position as a wedding planner for a company that specializes in organizing weddings. She might want to be supervised closely as she plans her first few events. An effective humble leader knows when the time is right to back off from micromanagement and shift to macro-management.

A LEADER WITH HUMILITY: CHRIS COX, CHIEF PRODUCT OFFICER AT FACEBOOK

Chris Cox is the chief product officer at Facebook. Since 2021, Facebook Inc.'s total family of apps and technologies has been placed under the brand, Meta. His key role is to determine how the various units of Facebook fit together, and handle conflicts as groups compete for attention and resources. Another major responsibility for Cox is to run the Facebook social network itself.

Cox is known for his ability to carefully guide the introduction of new products as well as for his superior ability to engage in warm interpersonal relationships with his team as well as other Facebook employees. He is also well-liked by financial analysts who meet periodically with the Facebook executive team. Cox has become a pitchman in company videos about Facebook presented to analysts. Cox has had many original ideas but gives considerable credit to his close work associates, "Team Cox."

Cox is also known for his hearty laugh, compassion, and humility. Meta employees often see him conduct walking meetings around the campus or riding to work alongside lower-ranking employees. Numerous company employees regard Cox as the embodiment of Meta's heart and soul.

Facebook founder and CEO, Mark Zuckerberg, says Cox is one of his closest friends, and also an individual who has made the company a really special place. Zuckerberg makes note of Cox's cognitive skills and emotional intelligence. He said, "It's really rare to find people who are very good at both." Facebook director of engineering Mark Slee, once said, "One of Chris' biggest skills is emotional intelligence. He's just one of those rare people from an engineering background who excels at that." Cox's high emotional intelligence has been useful in building cordial, constructive relationships with work associates.

At one point, Cox served as Facebook's first human resources chief. In this role he helped establish the Facebook culture, as well as defining the company's mission: "To make the world more open and connected." As a Facebook leader, Cox strives to make the company more social by encouraging positive interactions among employees. He also stays on top of product details such as trying to perfect the "Like" function.

Despite his amiable nature, Cox left Facebook in March 2019 amid disagreements with Zuckerberg over the company's strategic direction. A major point of disagreement was Zuckerberg's plans to move toward unifying Facebook's products around encrypted messaging. Cox worried that the move to encryption would hamper detection of criminal activity including terrorism and child trafficking. He also championed an effort within Facebook to scrutinize the company's culpability in spreading disinformation and divisive content.

In June 2020, Cox returned to Facebook, stating how he had been "encouraged by progress on many of the issues facing us." During his year away from the company, Cox spent part of his time working on politically progressive causes. Upon his return Cox was assigned oversight of the company's largest products: Facebook, Instagram, WhatsApp, and Messenger.[12]

GUIDELINES FOR ACTION

1. Humility is a critical behavior that leaders need to develop and communicate to establish connectivity with the team. As a humble leader, it will be easier for you to connect with your team.

2. "Being connected" to others involves many specific behaviors. Two examples are complimenting the actions of team members that please you, and helping employees understand the purpose of the organization and their work.

3. Humble leadership is well suited to building personal relationships because subordinates feel appreciated and understood.

4. The expression of gratitude is a robust method of demonstrating humility. The more effective form of gratitude is "other praising" rather than focusing on the self-benefit. An example: "You go out of your way to help during crunch time."

5. Discretionary rewards are useful in recognizing good performance. A discretionary reward is an honor where a manager, under no obligation, chooses to reward noteworthy behavior that goes beyond what is expected.

6. Informal recognition is a useful method for the leader to express gratitude. Describing what the worker did right is often more effective than merely making an evaluation. For example, "You did a great job with that angry customer."

7. A robust way for the humble leader to help group members grow and develop is to be a model of job-related learning. Learning with the group members can be helpful, such as in making a joint sales call.

8. Coaching with humility is a major strategy for building relationships with group members. Two of many examples is to give on-the-spot positive feedback as warranted, and to give emotional support.

9. Humble leaders can often build effective relationships with group members through reverse mentoring, or being taught something specific from a younger group member. Reverse mentoring is not confined to computer technology, and can include many other skills and knowledge.

10. Leaders with humility take naturally to avoiding micromanagement because they usually assume that the person performing a task has more job-relevant knowledge than they do. Instead, humble leaders macro-manage when appropriate, meaning they still offer advice and guidance when needed.

NOTES

1. Beth Coleman, "Humility: A Leadership Trait That Gets Results," *Leadership Spotlight* (https://leb.fbi.gov/spotlights), March 5, 2014, p. 1.

2. Edgar H. Schein and Peter A. Schein, *Humble Leadership: The Power of Relationships, Openness, and Trust* (New York: Berrett-Koehler, 2018).

3. "Five Factors That Define Connectivity in both Leadership and Business," *Inscape* (www.inscapeconsulting.com), © 2020, pp. 1–4; Roger Trapp, "Why Successful Leadership Depends on Connections," *Forbes* (www.forbes.com), May 26, 2015, pp. 1–3.

4. Heidi Grant, "Stop Making All About You," *Harvard Business Review* (hr.org), June 20, 2026, pp. 1–4.

5. Jana Gallus, "The Best Ways to Give Employees Performance Awards." *The Wall Street Journal*, October 30, 2018, p. R9.

6. Bradley P. Owens and David R. Hekman, "Modeling How to Grow: An Inductive Examination of Humble Leader Behaviors, Contingencies, and Outcomes," *Academy of Management Journal*, August 2012, pp. 787–818.

7. Marcus Buckingham and Ashley Goodall, "The Feedback Fallacy," *Harvard Business Review*, March–April 2019, pp. 92–101.

8. Marilyn J. Darling, "Coaching Helps People through Difficult Times," *HR Magazine*, November 1994, p. 72.

9. Christopher Lochhead, "3 Lessons in Humble Leadership from Four-Star General Stanley McChrystal," *growwire.com*, October 10, 2018, pp. 1–2.

10. Jeff Kirschner, "Humility and Leadership," *RHR International* (www.rhrinternational), October 30, 2018, pp. 1–2.

11. Jess Johnson, "Humility in Leadership: Battling the Vices of Pride," *Crowdstaffing* (www.crowdstaffing.com) May 1, 2018, p. 3.

12. Original story based on facts and observations in the following sources: Salvador Rodriguez, "If Mark Zuckerberg is Facebook's Brain, Chris Cox Is Its Heart, Employees Say," *CNBC* (cnbc.com), February 7, 2021, pp. 1–11; Jeff Horwitz, "Executive Returns To Facebook After A Zuckerberg Rift," *The Wall Street Journal*, June 12, 2020, pp. B1, B4; Jessica Guynn, "Facebook's Chris Cox: A Very Likeable Pitchman," *Los Angeles Times* (http://articles.latimes.com), May 12, 2012, pp. 1–3; Josh Constine, "Facebook Promotes VP Of Product Chris Cox to Chief Product Officer, But No Organizational Change, " *TC* (https://techcrunch.com), May 2, 2014, pp. 1–7.

6

Practices of Humble Leaders and Professionals

Closely related to the attributes and skills of humble leaders and professionals and the components of humility are the practices they use to carry out their jobs. Assume that product manager Amy has good listening skills as part of her humility. These listening skills might translate into Amy taking a *listening tour* of employees and customers when she is assigned a new product to manage. In this chapter we look at 12 actions often used by humble leaders and professionals as they engage in their professional roles.

PRACTICING OPEN-HANDED LEADERSHIP

As stated by business writer Eric Torrence, leadership is not about having a monopoly on great ideas. Instead, the most effective leaders have a knack for finding the latest and greatest ideas. In this sense they practice *open-handed leadership* because they humbly keep their hands open for gathering useful ideas from others. Torrence points out that in a quickly changing world, leaders who have lasting impact understand the importance of being adaptable.

Part of this adaptability is to recognize that innovative thinking can come from unexpected sources. A humble leader listens attentively to suggestions from people at any job level about suggestions for improvement. For example, the director of e-commerce at a retailer or business-to-business enterprise might listen to an entry-level worker about how to reduce the amount of protective material that is placed in a shipping

DOI: 10.4324/9781003461784-6

box. Adaptability can also mean a leader or professional's willingness to let go of an idea whose time has passed. John S. Chen, the longtime CEO of Blackberry Limited, recognized around 2018 that the days of the BlackBerry mobile phone were over despite its past prominence. Chen then shifted the company into reliance on enterprise software, the Internet of Things, and artificial intelligence.

Open-handed leaders, in short, understand their limited perspective. They recognize that new trends, different generations and generational preferences, and changing dynamics impact all fields.[1]

PRACTICING HANDS-ON LEADERSHIP

Open-handed leadership and hands-on leadership sound alike but they are not the same thing. The hands-on leader works quite closely with group members in solving problems, and will contribute expertise of his or her own. Authoritarian leaders and humble leaders practice a hands-on approach for different reasons. The authoritarian leader often thinks he or she knows best how to accomplish the tasks of the group. In contrast, the humble leader practices hands-on leadership because he or she does not feel beyond working closely with group members.

During John's time as a naval officer he learned the value of walking down the bridge to where the work of the ship was happening. He referred to this practice as "walking the deck plates." The people closest to the work being performed by the group appreciate the leader not being out of touch with the challenges and technical details of the work. As part of this hands-on approach to leadership, workers provide the leader with useful insights and ideas that might strengthen the leader's influence.[2] For example, the leader might learn that a piece of equipment is approaching obsolescence and should be replaced. After the leader obtains the new equipment, the unit performs better and the leader becomes more influential.

Another advantage of hands-on leadership is that the head of the unit works together with team members to find solutions to problems. A team will often look forward to a leader whose humility enables him or her to work directly with the team and not strictly for the leader.[3] For example, during a crisis such as the coronavirus pandemic, a chief financial officer might work closely with the team to find a way the company can raise money to stay afloat until normal business activity resumes.

APPROPRIATE USE OF AUTHORITY

In the words of psychologist Sherrie Campbell, "We are the most repulsed by loud, egotistical authority figures who lead from narrow-mindedness, my-way-or-the-highway fear tactics, shame, threats, and intimidation to get the results they want." Using a much different approach, humble leaders do not use their rank as a platform to abuse. They take a balanced approach to authority to encourage others, and to delegate authority and responsibility to people capable of doing the work. Humble leaders function somewhat like a player-coach, a person who has both playing and coaching responsibilities. They use their position of authority to establish order and discipline among team members. Humble leaders are on the front lines helping the team to recognize and pursue their individual and collective goals.[4]

As stated by researcher Rahul Eragula, true success takes place when authority meets humility. An arrogant manager or leader will often have difficulty in delegating effectively.[5] The effectiveness problem occurs because the arrogant leader pushes all the responsibility on group members yet retains all the authority. An example of responsibility without authority would be when a group member has the responsibility for dealing with a surge in demand yet lacks the authority to hire additional workers either full-time or part-time. With humility, the leader is more comfortable granting authority to others.

LEADING BY EXAMPLE

Previously we described how humble leaders were a model of learning for group members. Humble leaders also lead by example by asking for help and listening to feedback from others. Such practices are then likely to be followed by many group members. A humble leader often leads by example by demonstrating that politeness and respect for others is an effective approach to interpersonal relations.

The humble leader by acting as a positive role model is able to exert influence in many ways. The ideal approach is to be a "do as I say and do" manager—that is, one whose actions and words are consistent. Actions and words confirm, support, and often clarify each other. Being respected facilitates leading by example because group members are more likely to follow the example of leaders they respect. A major way in which a leader obtains respect is by being trusted. Part of the respect Apple CEO Tim Cook has received is that he can be trusted to follow through on his plans such as acquiring companies to help Apple grow and paying dividends to investors to provide an additional reward for investing in the company.

Leading by example is often interpreted to mean that the leader works long and hard, and expects others to do the same, with this type of behavior being prevalent among entrepreneurs who hire staff. During the startup phase of a company, the entrepreneur will often work over 60 hours per week and expect the new hires to follow a similar work schedule. A humble leader, however, is less likely to be work-obsessed and expects group members to emulate his or her behavior. A humble leader is more likely to make reasonable demands on constituents.

CONDUCTING A LISTENING TOUR

A humble leadership practice that has become almost standard is for a newly appointed, high-level leader to tour his or her area of responsibility and listen to workers, and perhaps customers. The tour helps establish rapport with constituents and also demonstrates that the leader cares about the workers' concerns. A bold humble approach is to casually ask workers what problems he or she should tackle first as the new leader.

A representative case example is that of Emily Guthro who started a new job as a human resources manager at Goodwill in Hamilton, Ontario. She wanted to make sure her first days on the job were well spent, and she also had a genuine interest in the well-being of staff members. Her decision was to conduct a listening tour that involved a one-on-one meeting in person with the head of each department. She developed a list of questions that she would ask each person, and listened carefully to the responses.

Although Guthro said she had not heard of middle managers doing a listening tour, she was encouraged by her new boss when had done this when he began in a new role. Guthro emailed her questions in advance of the face-to-face meetings. "I wanted to get the lay of the land and learn about the different personalities, the needs of the various business units, and a feel for the culture," said Guthro. The meetings helped trigger a connection with key people she would be serving within Goodwill. Guthro emphasized that it is important to build bridges and make sure you are not merely a name on the organization chart. It is also essential to put a face to the people and positions you will be serving.[6]

The listening tour is the most likely to project humility when the leader emphasizes listening rather than providing a preview of his or her ideas and plans. This is particularly true because a humble leader would gather input from many people before formulating plans for making changes. The listening tour may be effective but it is still a preliminary attempt at building rapport and obtaining valuable input about organizational problems. The new leader will have to establish trust before workers open up about what changes in the organization or unit of the organization, they think are necessary.

HELPING OTHERS BECOME SELF-SUFFICIENT

A leadership practice embraced by humble leaders is to help others grow, develop, and become more self-sufficient. Instead of creating a dependency on him or her, the humble leader finds ways to help others function more independently. Among the many ways a leader might develop self-sufficiency in others would be to give them challenging assignments, and provide positive feedback and constructive criticism. The following scenario illustrates how a leader might contribute to the self-sufficiency of a subordinate. Aldo is the hotel manager, and Chelsea is the assistant manager.

Aldo: I will be away the last seven days in June to attend a corporate meeting. You will be the acting hotel manager during my absence.

Chelsea: Thanks for the chance to be acting manager. That's a lot of responsibility during the beginning of the height of the tourism season.

Aldo:	I know that managing the hotel is a lot of responsibility. I consider myself lucky to have a competent person like you in charge during my absence.
Chelsea:	I know that I will be in charge, but you are still the true hotel manager.
Aldo:	You are right. My name will still be on the organization chart and at the end of the reservation counter. But you will be the leader of the hotel while I am away.
Chelsea:	Okay, but I assume that I can send you text messages whenever I need your opinion on a problem or a tough decision.
Aldo:	Please do get in touch with me if we have a fire or flood, but otherwise just an occasional message about how well things are going.
Chelsea:	Have a nice trip and don't worry about anything. I will be in charge.
Aldo:	You got that right.

TOLERATION OF AMBIGUITY

In recent years, as the world of work has become more uncertain and rapidly changing, the ability to tolerate ambiguity as well as thrive from it has gained in importance for leaders and individual contributors. Furthermore, the complexity of problems in the workplace makes clear-cut answers elusive. Tolerating ambiguity means that you can capitalize on situations that are somewhat vague and lacking in structure. "You manage the gray" because you recognize that tough and complex decisions are not black and white.

A major reason that humble leaders and professionals tolerate ambiguity better than most people is that they recognize that they may not have an immediate answer to every problem they face. In contrast, they understand that many problems do not have immediate answers but must be studied carefully, usually with input from others. A humble CEO, for example, might be facing a situation of losing market share. With humility, the leader thinks, "It is difficult to understand clearly why we are losing market share. Before we jump in and lower prices to regain market share, let's study the situation. Products lose market share for many reasons. Let's investigate the problem as a team."

The accompanying self-quiz provides you with an opportunity to think about your tendencies toward tolerating ambiguity.

MY TENDENCIES TOWARD TOLERATING AMBIGUITY

Indicate your strength of agreement with each of the following statements: SD—*Strongly Disagree*; D—*Disagree*; N—*Neutral*, A—*Agree*; SA—*Strongly Agree*. Because the results of this quiz are not being used to evaluate you in any way, be as candid as possible.

Statement related to Tolerance for Ambiguity	SD	D	N	A	SA
1. It is okay with me if my boss does not give me a clear picture of what he or she wants done.	1	2	3	4	5
2. It really bothers me when I read an article, and the author does not present a conclusion.	5	4	3	2	1
3. If I am assigned a project, it is essential that I be given a due date.	5	4	3	2	1
4. I dislike so-called "impressionist" paintings because the people and objects in the painting are unclear.	5	4	3	2	1
5. I would enjoy it if I asked my boss a question, and he or she responded, "What do you think is the best answer."	1	2	3	4	5
6. It frustrates me when people speak to me in generalities.	5	4	3	2	1
7. My strong preference is for questions that can be answered either Yes or No.	5	4	3	2	1
8. The best employees engage in tasks only that fit their job description.	5	4	3	2	1
9. A major decision should be made only after almost all the relevant data have been gathered.	5	4	3	2	1
10. If I had 70 percent of the necessary facts, I would go ahead and make a decision.	1	2	3	4	5
11. With a little investigation, you can find the right way or wrong way to accomplish almost any task.	5	4	3	2	1
12. Some problems are almost impossible to solve.	1	2	3	4	5
13. I feel uneasy when I am placed in a room where I know almost nobody else.	5	4	3	2	1

Statement related to Tolerance for Ambiguity	SD	D	N	A	SA
14. When in a restaurant I am often willing to order a meal that I have never tasted before.	1	2	3	4	5
15. When taking a multiple-choice test, I become (or became) frustrated when one clear alternative did not stand out.	5	4	3	2	1
16. A major problem with the English language is that the same word can have several different meanings.	5	4	3	2	1
17. When I visit a medical office because of a health problem, I expect the medical professional to give me a precise diagnosis.	5	4	3	2	1
18. It frustrates me when a friend says he or she will meet me "around" a certain time.	5	4	3	2	1
19. It is essential for every state or province to have the same law about turning right on a red light.	5	4	3	2	1
20. I think it is well worth my time to study how to deal with ambiguity.	1	2	3	4	5

Scoring and Interpretation: Find your total score by summing the point values for each question.

85–100: You probably have a high tolerance for ambiguity which should be an asset to you in dealing with a variety of qualitative and quantitative problems as a leader or corporate professional.

70–84: You probably have a neutral, detached attitude toward tolerating ambiguity.

20–69: You probably have difficulty in dealing effectively with both qualitative and quantitative problems that you perceive to be ambiguous. To enhance your leadership and professional effectiveness, you might need to accept the reality that many of the problems you face are ambiguous in nature. At the same time, you might profit from learning to deal with such problems.

Note: A few items on this quiz are based on S. Budner, "Intolerance of Ambiguity as a Personality Variable," *Journal of Personality*, Volume 30, 1962, pp. 29–50, and A. O. Mac Donald Jr., "Revised Scale for Ambiguity Tolerance: Reliability and Validity," *Psychological Reports*, Volume 19, 1970, pp. 791–798.

A close look at the nature of ambiguity helps explain why a humble person can deal with it better. First, the information is too complex for the individual to understand easily. A person might be reading a report from an economist explaining that the net effect of increasing capital gains tax is to reduce the amount of revenue the government receives. The person becomes groggy trying to understand the economist's logic, and decides that the report is ambiguous. In response, the humble person might think, "I admit, it is difficult to understand some abstract ideas."

Second, the information is inadequate. A frequent problem with consumer-oriented websites is that the user is told to click on a particular tab to access specific information about his or her account. Unfortunately, the information is inadequate because the user is not told where on the website this tab can be found (and there are about ten tabs on the website where this subtab could possibly be found). A humble person might reflect, "I am having difficulty so I will seek help."

Third, the information is apparently contradictory. A directive from top-level management advises managers throughout the organization that a corporate downsizing will soon take place. Furthermore, employees who rank in the bottom 10 percent of performance will most likely be downsized. At about the same time, the HR vice president announces a program for helping poor performers get back on track through coaching and company-sponsored training. An ambiguity-intolerant manager might think that the company is establishing contradictory directives that will lead to chaos and confusion. An ambiguity-tolerant and humble manager might think, "In these uncertain times I will do the best I can to deal with the conflicting elements in this scenario."

In the words of British business writer, Adam Gale, "Tolerance of ambiguity will be a vital characteristic of leaders in the years to come. Chief executives cannot afford to bury their heads in the sand when the storms of uncertainty hit, because the storms will never cease."[7] Among the many ambiguities facing leaders at all levels are unclear job descriptions, unclearly stated customer expectations, and vague corporate strategies. For top-level leaders, uncertainties about the present and future economy present more ambiguity.

Ambiguity specialist David J. Wilkinson emphasizes that great leaders look for ambiguity, uncertainty, and risk. These leaders understand that the biggest payoffs will be found where there is uncertainty, and that exploring ambiguity is likely to reveal new opportunities.[8] Extreme examples of jumping into domains of ambiguity are the exploration of minerals in the North Pole region, and privatizing space travel. The outcomes of both ventures are uncertain, and the amount of money that will need to be invested can only be approximated.

Imagine that hotel manager Tamara along with her staff is facing a major disruptive change and the ambiguity brought about by such change. The hotel is located in downtown Boston, and has been suffering a steady decline in occupancy rates. Downtown is still a hub for business visitors and tourism, but an increasing number of homeowners and large apartment dwellers are renting space to tourists. The home office of the hotel chain is heavily concerned about the declining occupancy rate, and staff members down to the housekeepers have expressed worry about their employment.

Tamara has enough humility to be uncertain whether renting out living quarters is just a fad that will soon fade, or a permanent threat to downtown hotels, but she decides to start taking action. She sends out confident messages in person, by email, and through texting that the hotel is aware of the new competition from "unlicensed hotels." Tamara says that she, along with the hotel staff and corporate headquarters is up to the challenge of the low-price competition. She assures the staff that the hotel is a Boston institution and that a temporary downturn in business is only a bump in the road toward regaining the hotel's former glory. Tamara also informs people that the legality of renting space in a private home is still under review.

Tamara explains that the hotel is developing a tangible plan that will make staying in a stranger's house seem like a third-rate alternative. She talks about upgrading the hotel's technology offering for guests (such as advanced video conference and smart rooms) and finding ways to make reduced hotel rates profitable without laying off any staff members. Tamara says with enthusiasm, "Our elegant hotel, combined with superior service from our marvelous staff will keep our hotel a permanent fixture in downtown Boston."

Tamara has tolerated and managed humility well. She also displays the optimism often characteristic of humble leaders.

PLACING OTHERS IN THE SPOTLIGHT

A key reason that leaders with humility place others in the spotlight is that they find joy in the success of others, similar to parents who find joy in the success of their children. Humble leaders also believe that the success of group members is not a threat to their own identity as a leader. A positive consequence is that the leader is willing to promote others and to celebrate the achievements of team members.[9]

Susan Brust is the senior vice president and director of new product development for Nordic Ware. She is recognized as having an advanced ability to allow others to shine as leaders themselves. Her humble leadership approach has several key elements. First, she gives many people an opportunity to lead. Brust leads by surrounding herself with good people and then finding ways to let them come to the forefront. She says that rather than leading by "pulling people along," she leads by "pushing people ahead." When a variety of people are given the responsibility to step up, action moves forward.

Second, Brust acknowledges what the whole person brings to the table. In addition to acknowledging good work performance, she makes a point to acknowledge Nordic Ware employees for who they are as human beings. Sometimes this means that Brust has to overcome her introverted tendencies and engage in everyday workplace small talk that can reveal a lot about the non-work side of people. Brust does this because it helps her build deeper connections, particularly with employees who are not her direct reports.

Third, she accepts acknowledgment and credit from others. Shrugging off a compliment, such as saying "No big deal" downplays the relevance and judgment of the compliment giver. Fourth, Brust does not assume that people know they are doing a great job. Receiving recognition from the leader gives group members the reassurance that their contribution is recognized. Fifth, Brust recognizes that when they shine, you shine. She understands that when subordinates perform well, the leader has contributed to their success.[10] Again, the humble leader does not see success as a zero-sum gain.

The most direct way for a leader to place others in the spotlight is to brag about their accomplishments to people outside and inside the group. Yet bragging too strongly to insiders about the accomplishments of one team member has the potential to create feelings of rivalry. A prototypical example of bragging about a team member would be when a team leader says to his manager, "We never would have had this breakthrough with the creative thinking of Bree."

ASKING FOR FEEDBACK AND HELP

Paulette Ashlin, an executive business coach, believes that humility is at the heart of great leadership. She therefore often coaches her clients to ask for help because it is the highest form of flattery and a compliment to others.[11] One perspective is that being truly humble means being able to receive constructive criticism. Leaders who welcome receiving feedback show that they are interested in continuing to grow and learn. Such behavior helps the team because it demonstrates the value of listening to different points of view and accepting valid points when they are made.[12]

A frequent practice of humble leaders is that they regularly ask questions for two key reasons. First, they recognize that they do not have all the answers. Second, and even more importantly, they recognize that asking group members questions helps them grow professionally. Journalist Warren Berger has devoted much of his writing career to the power of questions. He strongly recommends that questioning be a regular practice among leaders. One question that leaders should ask every day is "How can I help?"[13]

Asking for help is part of humility, yet when overdone might suggest that the leader is having difficulty carrying out his or her role. A humble but still strong way of asking for help yet still appearing up the job would be, "I would like your input into this challenging problem." A humble but weak-appearing way of asking for help would be, "I am in over my head. Can you figure this out for me?"

ACCEPTING COMPLIMENTS

As mentioned above by Nordic Ware CEO Susan Brust, a humble leader accepts compliments graciously. It has been observed that when humble leaders are complimented, they feel comfortable and worthy of the compliment. Instead of discounting the compliment, they typically say, "Thank you for taking the time to share that feedback with me. I appreciate that." Leaders with high self-confidence know that if they do not feel worthy enough to accept compliments, others inside and outside the group will stop giving them.[14]

When receiving compliments, a leader with humility still has to sort out genuine compliments versus those lodged simply to gain political advantage. Leadership consultant John Addison reminds us that the further you rise in an organization, the more people you have telling you how great you are because of your effect on the amount of money they make. A rule of thumb for assessing the legitimacy of a compliment is to ask yourself, "Is there anything I accomplished that in any way merits this compliment?"[15]

APOLOGIZING WHEN APPROPRIATE

Apologizing is a core component of the humble person, and humble leaders apologize appropriately when the situation warrants. An *appropriate* apology acknowledges a mistake but not in a self-demeaning, self-effacing manner. A CEO might state during a town hall meeting,

> *We bought this competitor for $1 billion two years ago. It proved to be a terrible drain on profitability, and we sold the company last month for $200 million. I apologize for having wasted so much of our corporate resources. It was a costly mistake that your executive team will never repeat.*

An effective apology includes an acknowledgment of wrongdoing, regret, responsibility for what happened, and a plan to remedy the problem.[16] The CEO who spearheaded the failed acquisition might therefore have also said, "I made an error in judgment, and I regret having wasted corporate money. It was my bad decision. Any acquisition we make in the future will be based on wider input from our management team and employees." Notice the use of "I" in the apology. Apologies are the most effective when stated in the first person, such as "I'm very sorry for what happened."

An apology perceived to be sincere is much more likely to be accepted. A research study verified the logical notion that followers who perceived their leader as trustworthy or caring before his or her wrongdoing were more likely to perceive their leader's apology to be sincere. Followers who previously doubted their leader's trustworthiness and caring were less likely to perceive the apology as sincere. Leaders and professionals with humility tend to be perceived as trustworthy and caring which suggests that their apologies are more stand a good chance of being accepted.

The study also suggested that leaders whose apologies appeared to be sincere were more likely to be perceived as humble.[17] It appears then that being humble makes your apologies more believable, and that believable apologies contribute to a perception of being humble!

PROMOTING DIVERSITY AND INCLUSION

A key practice of leaders with humility is to promote cultural diversity and inclusion. Humble leaders welcome diverse people and value each member of their teams. Cultural and demographic diversity refers to having a variety of cultures and statistically identifiable groups in the organization such as different races, ethnic groups, sexes, ages, and sexual orientations. *Inclusion* refers to being accepted, and welcomed, and for people to feel that they belong to the organization. An organization might be diverse, without making an effort to reach out to its diverse members.

Inclusion goes one step beyond diversity because the different groups are overtly welcomed and included in making important decisions and social activities. A humble leader, for example, would work toward assuring that some elderly people and Native Americans in the organization hold key jobs and are part of the social network within the firm.

In addition to promoting inclusion, humility boosts diversity in another way because humility creates space for improvement. As described by diversity consultant DeEtta Jones, a diverse workplace brings different people together, and a humble leader understands that he or she has much to learn about people who are different.[18] For example, a humble leader might reflect, "Kato is from Thailand. English is her second language. So, I will minimize idioms and sports analogies when we are communicating about work-related problems."

Management consultants Juliet Bourke and Andrea Espedido conducted research on inclusive leadership. A major finding was that what leaders say and do makes about a 70 percent difference in whether an employee reports feeling included. In support of the present discussion, a signature trait of these inclusive leaders is humility. The trait was defined in the study as being modest about capabilities, admitting mistakes, and creating the space for others to contribute.

The study also found that leaders who are humble acknowledge their vulnerability to bias, and therefore ask for feedback on their blind spots and habits. One direct report told the researchers, "My leader is very open and vulnerable about her weaknesses, which she mentions when we undergo team development workshops. She shares her leadership assessments openly with the team and often asks for feedback and help to improve."[19]

A LEADER WITH HUMILITY: ARNOLD DONALD, THE FORMER CEO OF CARNIVAL CORP

Arnold W. Donald was the CEO of Carnival Corp., the world's largest travel company. Donald was the former chairman of the chemical company, Merisant, and a top executive at the weed killer division of Monsanto. He became CEO of Carnival Corp. in 2013 after having served on the Board for 13 years. In 2022, he stepped down from his roles as CEO and Board member after 21 years of service to the cruise line. He then shifted to a consulting role where he continued to provide counsel and advice to the company.

When Donald shifted to a consulting role, Micky Arison, Chair of the Board of Directors praised his leadership and success in these words:

> *He leads by example, listens intently, acts with integrity, and puts a strong emphasis on supporting everyone around him. Arnold connects deeply with people and has an extraordinary ability to communicate, which makes him one of the most important and influential voices in our industry.*

Donald was the first African-American CEO in the travel industry. When Donald became CEO, Carnival was reeling from several crises, including a deadly ship crash and a ship idled in the ocean in an unsanitary condition. One of Donald's major goals was to increase the percentage of North Americans who cruise each year, which has stood at 4 percent for many years.

In terms of his position, Donald is a powerful executive. At the same time, he leads with humility as evidenced by his penchant for listening to employees and encouraging diversity of thought. Donald spent his first few months as CEO of Carnival listening carefully to employees. He said with humility, "If you listen to your employees that do all the work, they'll tell you how to executive."

Because Donald took over at a difficult period, he saw the importance of building employee morale. To accomplish this end, he pulled his top team together and said, "What does success look like for you and your family five years from now? What does success look like for you and your department? Now share that with each other." Donald said he wanted to get listening established in the organization.

In terms of anticipating the desires of sophisticated customers, Donald focuses on feedback. Carnival has real-time feedback continually. He says that Carnival listens to its guests, and particularly emphasizes listening to employees.

Donald is a strong believer in what he labels as Diversity in Thinking. "The only way businesses thrive over time is through innovation," he says,

> *Innovation, by definition, is thinking outside the box. If you bring people together from different backgrounds and different cultural experiences who are organized around a common objective, you're far more likely to create breakthrough innovation than a homogeneous group.*

To achieve Diversity in Thinking, Donald practices cultural diversity in his management team. Within his first three years as CEO, Donald replaced seven of the nine heads of the cruise line brands at Carnival Corp. Four of the present brand heads are women. Donald also recruited Orlando Ashford, an African-American to run Holland America. Ashford's background was in human resources, not travel or cruise ships. From Arnold's perspective, "Diversity of thinking is a business imperative and a powerful advantage."

By the third quarter of 2020, Carnival Corp. was still facing the crisis created by the lingering coronavirus shutdown. A troublesome development for Carnival is that the cruise line had been at the center of several high-profile onboard outbreaks. One example is that the Diamond Princess was quarantined at a Japanese port in one of the first major outbreaks outside of China. Donald remained optimistic, saying that the cruise industry would bounce back along with the rest of the travel industry. The company reported a $4.4 billion second-quarter loss, and management could not predict when operations would resume. A few months earlier Donald stated that bookings for 2021 were brisk. Donald believed that he and other company employees would rise to the occasion of restoring the prominence of Carnival. The company continues to prosper today.[20]

GUIDELINES FOR ACTION

1. A straightforward way of being a humble leader is to practice open-handed leadership, or readily gathering and accepting ideas from others. Open-handed leadership gives you the opportunity to gather ideas from unexpected sources.

2. Hands-on leadership provides you with a good opportunity to work together with team members to find solutions to problems.

3. An effective practice for a humble leader is to occupy the role of a player-coach, a person who has both playing and coaching responsibilities.

4. It is consistent with humble leadership by acting as a positive role model in many ways, or leading by example.

5. A standard approach for a newly appointed leader is to take a listening tour. To practice humble leadership during the tour, it is particularly important to emphasize listening and gathering information rather than discussing your upcoming plans.

6. A robust approach to humble leadership is to help others become more self-sufficient rather than creating a dependency relationship with the leader.

7. Tolerating ambiguity is an effective humble leadership practice because humble leaders understand that many problems do not have immediate answers, but must be studied carefully, usually with input from others. When uncertainty exists, big opportunities may be forthcoming.

8. Placing others in the spotlight is a basic practice of humble leaders, and is based on finding joy in the accomplishments of others.

9. Asking others for help is another standard humble leadership practice, and is also the highest form of flattery and a compliment to others.

10. Part of humble leadership is being able to accept compliments graciously, and not to pretend that the compliment was not deserved.

11. Apologizing is a core component of the humble person, and humble leaders apologize appropriately when the situation warrants. Acknowledge a mistake, but not in a demeaning, self-effacing manner.

12. A key practice of leaders with humility is to promote cultural and demographic diversity, and inclusion. The latter refers to accepting and welcoming diverse people, and making them feel they belong to the organization.

NOTES

1. Eric Torrence, "Open-Handed Leadership: The Intersection of Humility, Adaptability, Longevity, and Influence," www.thindifference.com, 2020, pp. 1–3.
2. Skip Prichard, "How Leaders Can Be Humble in an Age of Arrogance," February 19, 2019, pp. 1–7.
3. Varun Saxena, "5 Ways to Bring More Humility in Your Leadership," *Your Story* (yourstory.com), August 29, 2018, pp. 1–2; Joseph Ottorino, "Four Leadership Lessons in Humility," *The Globe and Mail* (www.globeandmail.com), May 15, 2018, pp. 1–6.
4. Sherrie Campbell, "9 Reasons Humility Is the Key to Exceptional Leadership," August 24, 2017, pp. 1–4.
5. Rahul Eragula, "Humility in Leadership," *Advances in Economics and Business Management*, April–June 2015, p. 788.
6. Bill Kaiser, "Follow the Humble Leader," *High Performing Culture* (www.highper formingculture.com), © 2014–2019, p 1.
7. Adam Gale, "Managing Uncertainty: A Post-Brexit Guide for Leaders," *Management Today* (www.managementtoday.co.uk), December 2015, p. 1.
8. David J. Wilkinson, *The Ambiguity Advantage: What Great Leaders Are Great At* (New York: Palgrave Macmillan, 2006), p. 135.
9. Justin Flunder, "How Important Is Humility in Leadership?" *Country Sunrise News* (www.countrysunrisenews.com), April 24, 2014, p. 2.
10. Matt Norman, "5 Ways Humble Leaders Put Others in the Spotlight," www.matt normal.com, June 20, 2018, pp. 1–3.
11. "Leaders as Learners: Humility Is the Heart of Great Leadership (Interview with Paulette Ashlin)," www.globalgirlsproect.org, October 28, 2014, p. 7.
12. Adina Miron, "Leading with Humility: Five Golden Rules," eskill.com/blog, August 13, 2014, p. 1.
13. Warren Berger, *A More Beautiful Question: The Power of Inquiry to Spark Breakthrough Ideas* (New York: Bloomsbury, 2014).
14. Peter Barron Stark, "9 Habits of Humble Leaders," www.peterstar4k.com, July 7, 2016, p. 2.
15. "How to Be a Humble Leader," johnaddisonledership.com © 2019 Addison Leadership Group, INC.
16. Alina Tugend, "An Attempt to Revise the Lost Art of the Apology," *The New York Times* (http://nytimes.com) January 30, 2010, p. 1.

17. Tessa E. Basford, Lynn R. Otfermann, and Tara S. Behrend, "Please Accept My Sincerest Apologies: Examining Follower Reactions to Leader Apology," *Journal of Business Ethics*, January 2014, pp. 99–117.

18. DeEtta Jones, "The Importance of Humility to Diversity and Inclusion," www.detajones.com, June 27, 2018, pp. 1–3.

19. Juliet Bourke and Andrea Espedido, "The Key to Inclusive Leadership," *Harvard Business Review* (https://hbhr.org), March 6, 2020, pp. 1–6.

20. Original story based on facts and observations in the following sources: Melissa Mayntz, "Carnival Leadership Change: Major Board Member Stepping Down," *Cruisehive* (www.cruisehive.com), November 3, 2022, pp. 1–5; William Feuer, "Carnival CEO: Despite 'Devastating' Coronavirus Outbreak, Cruise Bookings for 2021 Are Strong," *CNBC* (www.cnbc.com) April 14, 2020, pp. 1–4: John J Edwards III, "Carnival Reports $4.4 Billion Loss, Can't Predict Resumption," www.bloomberg.com, June 18, 2020, pp. 1–3; Vanessa Fuhrmans, "Carnival's CEO Steers Turnaround Effort," *The Wall Street Journal*, June 14, 2018, p. B5; Anne Moore, "Carnival CEO Arnold Donald '80, on the Power of Hospitality," *Chicago Booth Magazine* (www.chicagobooth.edu), October 10, 2018, pp. 1–4; Carmine Gallo, "The Nine Words That Took This CEO From Poverty To the Top Of a $48 B Company," *Forbes* (www.forbes.com), May 13, 2018, pp. 1–4

7

Servant Leadership and Humility

In years past it might have been acceptable for subordinates in service occupations to say, "I am your humble servant." Today it is acceptable for people in charge in many organizations to say, "I am your humble servant leader." Many effective leaders believe that their primary mission is to serve the needs of their constituents, including employees, customers, and communities. They measure their effectiveness in terms of their ability to help others.

Servant leaders have enough humility to see themselves as stewards of the organization who seek to grow the organizations physical, financial, and human resources. Servant leaders operate from the motivation, "I serve" rather than "I lead." The observation has been made that humility might be the operating mechanism through which servant leaders function.[1] It takes humility to want to serve others.

A servant leader, as with other humble leaders, emphasizes ethical behavior, and high-quality relationships with group members. The term *servant leader* was coined in 1970 by Robert Greenleaf who stated that leaders serve followers, and great leaders are servants first.[2] Kathleen Patterson later provided a definition of servant leadership that points to what an ideal version of such a leader does in practice: Servant leadership means "leading by truly loving your followers, walking with humility. Doing the right things for people, being a visionary for your followers, trusting in others, empowering others, all the while leading with a heart to serve."[3]

Another way humility is linked to servant leadership is that servant leaders tend to be humbled by the cause they serve.[3] The CEO of a waste removal company, for example, might think, "I am humbled to help keep the planet cleaner and sustainable."

DOI: 10.4324/9781003461784-7

Before we dig further into servant leadership, you are invited to take the accompanying self-quiz to think about yourself as a present or potential servant leader.

THE SERVANT LEADERSHIP QUIZ

Indicate your strength of agreement with each of the following statements in relation to any leadership experience you have had. If you do not have leadership experience, imagine how you would respond to the actions and attitudes mentioned. SD—*Strongly Disagree*; D—*Disagree*; N—*Neutral*, A—*Agree*; SA—*Strongly Agree*. Because the results of this quiz are not being used to evaluate you in any way, be as candid as possible.

Statement related to Servant Leadership	SD	D	N	A	SA
1. I am interested in each group member as a person.	1	2	3	4	5
2. I enjoy being a leader because of the power the position brings me.	5	4	3	2	1
3. My intent is to create high ethical standards within the group.	1	2	3	4	5
4. What my group accomplishes is more important than the welfare of our members.	5	4	3	2	1
5. I give group members the authority to do their job.	1	2	3	4	5
6. I encourage group members to tell me how they contribute to the organization's vision.	1	2	3	4	5
7. A major part of my role is to help each member of the group succeed.	1	2	3	4	5
8. A key part of my job as a leader is to help each member of the team perform his or her job well.	1	2	3	4	5
9. A major responsibility of my group is to make me look good as a leader.	5	4	3	2	1
10. I see myself as a leader providing a useful service to group members.	1	2	3	4	5
11. I give group members the information they need to perform their jobs well.	1	2	3	4	5
12. I encourage group members to use their talents.	1	2	3	4	5
13. An important part of my role as a leader is to collect useful ideas from the group.	1	2	3	4	5

Statement related to Servant Leadership	SD	D	N	A	SA
14. I stay in the background and give credit to individual group members.	1	2	3	4	5
15. My personal success is more important to me than the success of group members.	5	4	3	2	1
16. It would make me proud to be labeled a "servant leader."	1	2	3	4	5
17. I see myself more as a mentor and coach than an authoritarian leader.	1	2	3	4	5
18. I learn from the criticism I receive from group members.	1	2	3	4	5
19. I tend to ignore whiners and complainers in the group.	5	4	3	2	1
20. I enjoy helping group members resolve difficult work-related problems.	1	2	3	4	5

Scoring and Interpretation: Find your total score by summing the point values for each question.

85–100: You probably practice servant leadership to a high degree. You may occasionally need to assert yourself more as a leader, and recognize that it is important to exercise your authority.

70–84: You probably have or would have a constructive approach to being a servant leader.

20–69: You probably have difficulty or would have difficulty engaging the role of a servant leader. Perhaps you could incorporate more aspects of servant leadership into your leadership style.

Note: The idea behind a few of the statements in this quiz stems from the following sources: Dirk van Dierendonck and Inge Nuijten, "The Servant Leadership Survey: Development and Validation of a Multidimensional Measure," *Journal of Business and Psychology,* September 2011, pp. 249–267; Robert S. Dennis and Mihal Bocarnea, "Development of the Servant Leadership Assessment Instrument," *Leadership & Organization Development,* December 2005, pp. 600–615.

KEY ASPECTS OF SERVANT LEADERSHIP

The idea of servant leadership may seem straightforward, yet servant leadership encompasses many different components including behaviors and attitudes on the part of the leader.[4] Furthermore, servant leadership might be regarded as complex as humble leadership.

1. *Place Service Before Self-Interest.* A servant leader is more concerned with helping others than with acquiring power, prestige, financial reward, and status. The servant leader seeks to do what is morally right, even if it is not financially rewarding. He or she is conscious of the needs of others and is driven by a desire to satisfy them. An example of a questionnaire item measuring this behavior is "My leader puts my best interests ahead of his or her own."[4] By placing service before self-interest, servant leaders might also be characterized as givers rather than takers. *Givers* are people who frequently give their time, effort, and resources to help others without expecting a return. *Takers* do the opposite by taking other people's time, effort, and resources with no intention of reciprocity.[5]

2. *Listen First to Express Confidence in Others.* The servant leader makes a deep commitment to listening in to get to know the concerns, requirements, and problems of group members. Instead of attempting to impose his or her will on others, the servant leader listens carefully to understand what course of action will help others accomplish their goals. After understanding others, the best course of action can be chosen. Through listening, for example, a servant leader might learn that the group is more concerned about team spirit and harmony than striving for companywide recognition. The leader would then concentrate more on building teamwork than searching for ways to increase the visibility of the team. Research suggests that the majority of servant leaders are introverted, facilitating their preference for listening.[6]

3. *Recognition of Own Limitations.* As with all humble leaders, servant leaders acknowledge their limitations and therefore actively seek the contributions of others to compensate for these limitations.[7] Servant leader and marketing manager Lance might say to

marketing assistant Brooklyn, "I'm not good at using big data to make a sales forecast for the next fiscal year. How about you taking over the task?"

4. *Boldness With Respect to Values, Morality, and Doing the Right Thing.* Humility is often associated with being overly modest, passive, and self-effacing. On the contrary, as noted by leadership scholar Jane T. Waddell, servant leaders can be very bold with respect to their sense of values, morality, and doing what is right.[8] These behaviors are part of the strong ethical code of most servant leaders. For example, a servant leader might insist that two people who are equally qualified for a position, have comparable experience and skills, and comparable performance are paid equally.

5. *Inspire Trust by Being Trustworthy.* Being trustworthy is a foundation behavior of the servant leader. He or she is scrupulously honest with others, gives up control, and focuses on the well-being of others. Usually, such leaders do not have to work hard at being trustworthy because they are already moral.

6. *Focus on the Development of People.* Servant leaders focus on the development of people, such as giving them an opportunity to acquire new skills and become leaders. The developmental focus requires humility in contrast to the politically motivated leader who prefers to avoid developing a person who might replace him or her.

7. *Focus on What Is Feasible to Accomplish.* Even though the servant leader is idealistic, he or she recognizes that one individual cannot accomplish everything. The leader therefore listens carefully to the array of problems facing group members and then concentrates on a few. The servant leader thus systematically neglects certain problems. A labor union official might carefully listen to all the concerns and complaints of the constituents and then proceed to work on the most pressing issue.

8. *Lend a Hand.* A servant leader looks for opportunities to play the Good Samaritan. As a supermarket manager, he or she might help out by bagging groceries during a busy period. Or a servant leader might help clean out the mud in the company lobby after a hurricane.

9. *Provide Emotional Healing.* A servant leader shows sensitivity to the personal concerns of group members, such as a worker being worried about taking care of a disabled parent. A recurring example

of the need for emotional healing is when a natural disaster, such as a tornado or sinkhole strikes an employee's home. The servant leader would likely grant the employee time off with pay to manage the problem, and also direct the employee toward any company resources available for emergency help.

10. *Act as a Role Model for Other Organizational Members to Emphasize Service.* As a result of the behaviors just described, servant leaders often ignite a cycle of service by acting as a role model of servant behavior. At his or her best, a servant leader helps establish a culture of serving others.

11. *Acquiring Power to Serve Others.* The motivation to acquire power is strong for leaders, particularly for those who aspire to an executive position. Servant leaders also like power but not for the purpose of self-aggrandizement. Instead, servant leaders seek power so the power can be used to serve the needs of constituents.[9] For example, a servant leader might want to acquire resources (a form of power) so he or she can create a pleasant and safe physical working environment for the workforce.

12. *Inverting the Organizational Pyramid.* From the perspective of organizational structure, servant leaders symbolically invert the traditional organizational structure. The CEO is placed at the bottom serving the other organizational members. Sameer Dholakia, the CEO of SendGrid, acknowledges that his job is difficult. He says, "But the folks doing the hard rowing of the business are not the CEO. I don't have to take a phone call from a customer who is upset about a bug. I don't have a sales quota."[10]

SERVANT LEADERSHIP AT THE RITZ-CARLTON

The Ritz-Carlton Hotel chain, a subsidiary of Marriott International, is acknowledged worldwide for its superior customer service. It makes sense that the company relies heavily on servant leadership because this approach to leadership emphasizes serving others. The Ritz-Carlton Motto is "We are Ladies and Gentlemen Serving Ladies and Gentlemen." The motto is designed to equalize not only employees to customers, but also every employee among each other.

To apply servant leadership, the following message is disseminated to hotel managers and other workers, "By applying the principle of trust, honesty, respect, integrity, and commitment, we nurture and maximize the benefit of each individual and the company."

The practice of servant leadership and outstanding customer service appears to have originated with Horst Schulze, the former president of the Ritz-Carlton Hotel Company. The late leadership authority Stephen R. Covey described Schulze as a very authentic person. His energy, commitment, and service to his people created a culture of serving. When Covey walked through the kitchen at the Ritz-Carlton at Amelia Island, he was amazed to find it was as clean as the lobby.

Schulze recalls being at the Five Stars Awards ceremony. Many of the great hoteliers from around the world were present. It was announced that Horst Schulze was in attendance, and everybody stood up and applauded. "But let's be honest, they didn't applaud me," said Schulze. "They applauded the image the Ritz-Carlton had built up, which was achieved by bellmen, doormen, busboy, cooks, waiters, maids and so on." (If Schulze were speaking today, the job titles just mentioned would be gender neutral, such as "door people" and "housekeepers.")

Schulze emphasized the Ritz-Carlton employees created the image of outstanding service. Company leadership created a great image that was good for everybody and good for employees. If a Ritz-Carlton employee conducts a job search, and there are a hundred other applicants, the Ritz-Carlton employee is chosen. Schulze believes that he was able to develop a strong positive reputation because of the many people doing a great job.

The motto also results in a flat rather than a hierarchical organization structure. Ritz-Carlton management believes it is more difficult to express humility when part of a hierarchical structure. Research suggests that servant leadership brings better job performance and service excellence in the hotel industry, and Ritz-Carlton leadership has taken these findings seriously.

At the Ritz-Carlton chain, front-office staff are not treated as instruments serving others. Instead, they are treated as equally valuable team members with important roles to carry out. A major aspect of servant leadership at the hotel is to incorporate a service-oriented climate into the organization. For example, a receptionist might observe a guest having a difficult time juggling the wheels on a suitcase. The receptionist would volunteer to help the customer make the proper adjustment.[11]

The Ritz-Carlton Hotel considers employees as its most significant asset. "At the Ritz-Carlton, our Ladies and Gentlemen are the most important resource in our service commitment to guests." The Employee Promise indicates, "By applying the principles of trust, honesty, respect, integrity and commitment we nurture and maximize talent to the benefit of each individual and the company."[12]

Herve Humler, who was part of the executive team at Ritz-Carlton that created its unique brand, became CEO in 2010. He emphasizes empowerment as part of his servant leadership, and reminds us that the Ritz-Carlton used the term *empowerment* long before it became a business buzzword. Empowerment is often manifested as the power of company employees to break away from the routine. Employees must seek out moments where a break from the routine brings value to the guest. Humler says,

> *If you are a server, you listen to the customer and if he or she expresses a desire for something different than what you are currently doing, you cater to it. If you are a maintenance engineer and you are painting the wall or changing a light bulb and the customer says "Hey, how are you? I need to get to the airplane." You can stop what you're doing and say, "Sir I am going to take you to the airplane."*

Humler emphasizes the service culture in a direct way. He says that it is his job, and the job of every leader in the organization, to remind those who work for us that we are not in the business of selling hotel rooms or food and beverage. Our hotels are in the business of selling exceptional service. He notes, "The privilege of serving our guests is the highest priority of the Ritz-Carlton Hotel Company. If we do that well, the rest of our job is easy and we will by default sell rooms."

Reflecting on his servant-leadership orientation, Humler says that his biggest joy is helping others succeed. He says that he has everything he wants in life, but through his great organization he is able to help the Ladies and Gentlemen succeed in so many ways for themselves and the Ritz-Carlton. "It is a gift I value and appreciate and an attribute I acknowledge as a sign of good leaders within our and other organizations."[13]

An aside about the extraordinary service climate at the Ritz-Carlton is that charging somewhere around $600 per night facilitates providing exceptional service. In turn, providing extraordinary service enables the hotel chain to charge $600 per night.

THE IMPACT AND EFFECTIVENESS
OF SERVANT LEADERSHIP

Servant leadership has attracted so much attention in recent years that many studies have been conducted about the impact and effectiveness of this style of leadership. Here we look at a few of the studies that help shed light on how being a servant leader and make a difference in an organizational unit, such as a team or department, or the entire organization.

Research evidence suggests that servant leadership at the top of the organization has a positive impact on the performance of a firm. The study involved 126 CEOs in the United States from the software and hardware technology industries. Servant leadership was measured by a self-report questionnaire, and firm performance was measured by return on assets (annual income divided by net assets). Analysis of data revealed that CEO servant leadership tendencies were significantly related to firm performance. Another part of the study suggested that CEOs who were company founders were more likely to be servant leaders,[14] reinforcing the idea that founders are often passionate about their company and its employees.

A study conducted in a large retail chain found that the leader's servant behavior is mirrored through co-worker modeling behavior and high-quality customer service.[15] A later study conducted in 71 restaurants of a restaurant chain found similar results. It was found that leaders created a serving culture in which the restaurant workers placed the needs of others before their own. The serving culture was positively related to the performance of the restaurants, as well as to individual job performance. Restaurant performance was measured by a composite of factors including carryout accuracy and customer satisfaction. Employee job performance was rated by managers, and included creativity and customer service behaviors.[16]

A study about servant leadership was conducted in 224 stores of a US retail organization, including 425 subordinates, 110 store managers, and 40 regional managers. Among the findings was that personality traits are related to being a servant leader. Leader agreeableness was positively related to servant leadership, but extraversion was negatively related. (Perhaps extraverted leaders do not listen enough to subordinates and tend to be self-centered.) Another finding of note was that servant leadership was associated with a higher degree of employee engagement and a lower degree of intention to quit.[16]

More evidence that servant leadership foster organizational citizenship behavior was found in a study conducted with seven multinational firms in Kenya, Africa. Participants in the study were 815 full-time employees from 123 different work groups. The results of the study provide insight into how servant leadership actually enhances citizenship behavior. Servant leadership appeared to foster a positive climate that in turn enhances organizational citizenship behavior.[17]

A study in a Quebec, Canada company that makes high technology products helps explain why servant leadership might lead to improved job performance and being a good organizational citizen. It was found that the servant leader's focus on employee development helps them satisfy the psychological needs for autonomy (working independently), competence, and relatedness (relating to other people). The satisfaction of these three needs fuels employees to perform better and be good organizational citizens.[18]

The sampling of different types of evidence suggests strongly that servant leadership can benefit group members, groups, and the organization. Yet an optimal level of servant leadership might still exist. At times, subordinates and the entire organization seek the guidance and inspiration of a decisive, action-oriented leader.

SUGGESTIONS FOR BECOMING A SERVANT LEADER

Suggestions for becoming a servant leader cover three useful possibilities. First, you are interested in becoming a servant leader. Second, you are already a servant leader but want to incorporate a few more servant leadership activities into your repertoire. Third, you are not interested in becoming a servant leader totally, but you want to touch lightly on becoming one by incorporating a few aspects of servant leadership into your style. All of the suggestions require a reasonable degree of humility to implement, including a willingness to benefit from the expertise of group members.[19]

1. *A Starting Point for Being a Servant Leader is to Ask the Group How You Can Best Help Them Within The Limits of Your Authority and Budget.* This approach is often incorporated into a listening tour when

a leader is newly appointed. Explaining that you have to work within the limits of your authority and budget helps reduce disappointed expectations. Among these disappointed expectations would be several group members thinking they merit a 25 percent increase in compensation, the group demanding that the company purchase the latest model supercomputer, or that the company should relocate. Asking how to help will often result in realistic expectations such as group members wanting to have more voice, or more time allocated to remote work.

2. *Ask How You Can Help Group Members Do Their Jobs Better, and Then Listen Mindfully.* Instead of telling people how you think they can perform their jobs better, ask them how you can help them perform more effectively. Offer your support and encourage group members to try new approaches to improving their work. Acting as a resource as to where help can be found is also an effective servant leadership approach. For example, as a leader you might be able to tap a company resource to help group members incorporate artificial intelligence (AI) into their business processes.

3. *Create Low-Risk Spaces for Group Members to Think of New Ideas.* An inhibitor to worker creativity can be a concern that if they come up with a new idea, and the idea bombs, they will be chastised. A practical way to create low-risk space would be for the leader to suggest to the team that they spend about 30 minutes in a huddle each Thursday afternoon to think of ways to reduce costs or increase revenues. Included would be the comment, "Let me know if you come up with anything good, but don't feel under pressure."

4. *If You Are a Company Founder, Build Servant Leadership into the Founding Values of the Enterprise.* The founder might begin by asking how he or she might create a better working environment for the people who are helping launch the new enterprise. Building in profit sharing or other ways to enable employees to share in the company's success is another contributor to implementing servant leadership.

5. *Stay Introspective About Your Strengths and Weaknesses.* When investing so much energy into the company or a unit thereof, it is easy to neglect keeping tabs on your own strengths and weaknesses. The true servant leader keeps on thinking about what he or she can do best, and where he or she needs the most help—following the dictates of humble leadership. For example, Lloyd, the founder of a

medical devices company, might reflect, "I have to remember that I have some natural talent as an inventor. But I know that a couple of other people on the team are much better at selling these inventions."

6. *Upend the Pyramid.* When your organization chart is the shape of a steep pyramid, with you at the top there are potential problems within the organization (We mentioned this point previously in reference to inverting the pyramid.) Kent Keith, the CEO of the Greenleaf Center for Servant Leadership, believes that people working in a steep hierarchy focus excessively on pleasing their bosses to the exclusion of doing the best for the customer. Also, the person at the top of the pyramid may not be receiving enough useful information. As a solution, Keith proposes forming a team at the top of the organization. The CEO still makes the final decisions, but creates a flatter structure with more openness to dialogue and dissent.

7. *Expand the Organizational Family.* Servant leadership also influences how suppliers and business partners are treated, not just customers and employees. Keith says, "Leaders of organizations should care about everyone that the organization touches (all the stakeholders)." The recommended approach is to make vendors and partners feel like part of the family by selling them on the importance of the company's mission. TD Industries, a mechanical construction company based in Texas, invites vendors to servant leadership training sessions the company holds for its staff.

8. *Have Your Team Monitor Your Activities Instead of the Other Way Around.* This point may be a bit exaggerated because a key part of the role of a leader or manager is to observe the performance of group members, and look for needed improvements. Nevertheless, to become a servant leader it is necessary to encourage feedback from subordinates. For example, a subordinate might say to the servant leader, "I appreciate all the freedom I have in my job, but it would help if you gave me more precise deadlines. A deadline helps me organize my work better."

9. *Focus on Giving Away Rather Than Accumulating Power.* The ultimate servant leader seeks to help others rather than accumulating power for personal use. As a result, the servant leader looks for ways to grant power to others through the standard techniques of delegation, empowerment, and participative decision-making. A

modest approach to giving away power is to give a group member an opportunity to take over your role when you are away on a business trip or vacation.

10. *Spend Some Time Every Day Connecting with Members of the Group Individually or Collectively.* Making connections with constituents is standard practice for effective leaders in general, but especially important for servant leaders. Most leaders face the temptation of spending all their time facing a computer screen, but such behavior does not reflect a helping, serving approach to the leadership role.

11. *Every Working Day Spend a few Moments Thinking About How You Can Add Value to the Group's Efforts.* Think of what you can do to help the group be successful. An effective question for a servant leader to ask is "What do you need from me today?"

12. *Facilitate Group Members Accomplishing their Work But Do Not Take Over Their Tasks.* An effective servant leader finds the fine line between facilitating task accomplishment for others versus doing tasks for them. Take the case of servant leader Anita, a bank manager. Clayton, one of the staff members, says that need needs help in figuring out how to convert Mexican pesos into US dollars, and the reverse. Clayton says, "Sure I can click on a computer tab, and have the software make the calculation for me, but it doesn't help me understand the process. Here is the currency conversion problem I am working on at the moment." Anita could do the calculation for Clayton, but instead, using a hand calculator, she shows him the arithmetic underlying converting pesos into dollars, and the reverse. Clayton has now learned a new skill.

13. *Recognize that All Jobs are Important.* Part of leadership humility is recognizing that every job in the organization contributes to its overall functioning. Stopping to ask people in various positions about the challenges they are facing shows recognition that every job is important. A city mayor with a servant-leadership orientation might ask the parking lot attendant who works the tollbooth, "What bottlenecks in the parking lot have you observed lately?"

14. *Remember the Details of What People Tell You.* An effective way of demonstrating that you want to help people and serve them is to remember details about what they told you during recent interactions. Having a sharp memory facilitates remembering details about what people told you, but taking notes on paper or electronically can be a

big assist. Ken, a distribution center manager, really impressed one of the forklift drivers he had not talked to in six months, when he said to the driver, "How much progress have you made with the arthritis in your left shoulder?" With his strong focus on people, Ken had jotted down a note on his phone six months ago about the forklift driver's troublesome shoulder.

A LEGENDARY SERVANT LEADER: KEN MELROSE, THE LATE CEO OF TORO

When Ken Melrose became CEO of the Toro Company in 1983 it was two years after the company had its worst year in revenues, posting its first loss in 35 years. (Melrose passed away on May 3, 2020.) Toro was burning so much cash that many financial analysts thought that the company could not be saved. Soaring interest rates and a recession hurt the company, and so did two winters with little snow that left the company with warehouses of unsold snowblowers.

Instead of being discouraged Melrose dug in and initiated drastic action. He reduced the size of the Toro workforce by 57 percent, cut executive perks, and sold a corporate jet. After these immediate salvage operations, Melrose tackled changing the corporate culture to an organization that empowered and trusted its employees, and placed a high value on workers. He used the term *bottom-up culture* to describe the new organizational culture.

During Melrose's time as Chairman and CEO, Toro's revenue grew dramatically, from approximately $250 million in 1983 to approximately $1.7 billion in 2005. Melrose said that the financial successes were merely by-products of doing what was right. (Doing what was right was combined with having high brand recognition and a high-quality product from a technical standpoint.) From a business perspective, Melrose strengthened the company by increasing the emphasis on lawn-care equipment for professional uses such as golf course maintenance and landscaping, and less on residential mowers. Professional equipment now constitutes about 80 percent of Toro's market.

Before taking over as CEO of Toro, Melrose was the head of a company subsidiary, Game Time, a playground equipment manufacturer. While at

Game Time, Morose observed three components of servant leadership. First, every employee has the potential to contribute and do good work. Second, this potential can be realized when the employee is "inspired, valued, engaged, empowered, and recognized." Third, the role of the leader is to create such an environment. When the leader at the top of the organization creates this environment, the company will attain its goals.

In talking about power, Melrose reveals how his concept of servant leadership has a strong religious bent. He says that real power comes to a leader when the person gives power to others. "This is how Jesus became powerful as an itinerant carpenter," he said. Melrose also believes that you lead best by serving the needs of your people. He added, "You don't do their jobs for them, you enable them to learn and progress on the job." Toro employees were also allowed to learn from failure without fear of reprisals, assuming that the mistake was not catastrophic.

The National Association of State Boards of Accountancy noted that through patience and longevity, Melrose demonstrated that running an organization with character and corporate soul can lead to financial success. Following his retirement as CEO of Toro and Chairman in 2006, Melrose created a company called Leading by Serving LLC, whose mission is to advance the principles of servant leadership in different types of organizations.

"The servant leadership model requires a change in attitude more than structure," Melrose said. "To operate in this model, leaders have to shed their egos and deeply embrace the belief that people perform best in an atmosphere of freedom and trust." Melrose was so passionate about servant leadership that he wrote the book, *Making the Grass Greener on Your Side: A CEO's Journey to Leading by Serving.* The book cited examples of servant leadership in practice at Toro. In addition. Melrose explained and encouraged its practice by others.

The Toro Company produces a full range of products in the landscape maintenance field. Several of the products, including lawnmowers and chainsaws can harm operators when mishandled or misused. A frequent industry practice when an operator was armed or killed using a lawn-care or snow removal product was to dispatch lawyers to quickly resolve the issue. The objective was to reach a quick financial settlement.

According to Ben Lichtenwainer, the founder of the leadership development firm Radiant Forest, Melrose had a different approach. Instead of sending legal teams, Toro sent counselors to help their customers in times of greatest need. The counselors helped injured customers cope with disabilities and survivors cope with loss. It was an approach that focused directly on the stakeholder and not on the stockholder or the Toro Company. Counseling injured customers substantially reduced legal costs and lawsuits. Instead of losing these users and their families. Toro found it made them lifelong, loyal customers. (Lichtenwainer comments that this is the empathy aspect of servant leadership in action.)

During his career, Melrose was a notable philanthropist. For example, Melrose made the largest single donation ever made to the Orange County Library System in Orlando, Florida, in 2012. "Both of my parents used to tell me that the purpose of life is to serve others," Melrose said. "My dad's way of serving was in the military. My mother's way of serving was in Orlando."[20]

GUIDELINES FOR ACTION

1. A useful starting point in becoming a servant leader is to emphasize ethical behavior, which in turn will help group members recognize that you are working in their best interests.
2. One of the most vital components of servant leadership is listening carefully to get to know the concerns, requirements, and problems of group members.
3. An easy-to-implement component of servant leadership is to acknowledge your limitations and seek the contribution of others to compensate for these limitations.
4. Another useful component of servant leadership is to focus on the development of group members such as giving them an opportunity to acquire new skills and become leaders.
5. If you are a servant leader at the top of an organization, you are likely to provide a positive model throughout the organization of service to others including customers.
6. Several studies have shown that introversion, or at least not exaggerated extraversion, is associated with servant leadership. To be a servant leader it is therefore helpful to sometimes emphasize the introverted side of your personality.

7. A useful early tactic for being a servant leader is to ask the group how you can help them within the limits of your authority and budget.

8. The true servant leader keeps on thinking about what he or she can do best, and where he or she needs the most help—following the dictates of humble leadership.

9. An effective way of being a well-rounded servant leader is to show care and concern for all stakeholders, not just employees and customers.

10. Every working day spend a few moments thinking about how you can add value to the group's efforts.

11. Part of being a servant leader is to recognize that all jobs are important, and that each one contributes to the overall functioning of the organization.

NOTES

1. J. Andrew Morris, Céleste M. Brotheridge and John C. Urbanski, "Bringing Humility to Leadership: Antecedents and Consequences of Leader Humility," *Human Relations*, No 10, 2005, p. 1339.

2. Robert K. Greenleaf, *The Servant Leader* (Newton Center, MA: The Robert K. Greenleaf Center, 1970).

3. Kathleen Patterson, "Servant Leadership and Love," in Dirk Van Dierendonck and Kathleen Patterson, *Servant Leadership* (London: Palgrave Macmillan, 2010).

4. Based on Robert K. Greenleaf, *Servant Leadership: A Journey into the Nature of Legitimate Power and Greatness* (Mahwah, NJ: Paulist Press, 1997); Robert C. Liden, Sandy J. Wayne, Hao Zhao, and David Henderson, "Servant Leadership: Development of a Multidimensional Measure and Multi-Level Assessment," *The Leadership Quarterly*, April 2008, pp. 161–177.

5. Cited in Rik Kirkland, "Wharton's Adam Grant on the Key to Professional Success," *McKinsey & Company* (www.mckinsey.com), June 2014, p. 3.

6. Jane T. Waddell, "Servant Leadership," *School of Leadership Studies Regent University* (www.regent.edu) August 2006, p. 3.

7. Dirk van Dierendonck and Inge Nuijten, "The Servant Leadership Survey: Development and Validation of a Multidimensional Measure," *Journal of Business and Psychology*, September 2011, pp. 249–267.

8. Waddell, "Servant Leadership," p. 3.

9. Milton de Sousa, "Humble Leaders Effective—Especially When in Power," https://discovery.rsm.nkl, June 19, 2014, p. 3.

10. Cited in Robyn Ward, "Great Leadership is about Humility and Serving, Not Ego and Directing," *The Startup* (https://medium.com) April 11, 2018, p. 1.

11. "Servant Leadership: Humility," *RitzCarltonleadershipCenter.com*, July 20, 2016, pp. 1–5; Stephen R Covey, "Examples of Servant Leaders," *Franklin Covey* (https:// resources.franklin.com/blog), © 2018, pp. 1–4; Darija Cviki, "Servant Leadership In AIRTH Encyclopedia of Innovation in Tourism and Hospitality," (www.airth .globasl), 2018.

12. Catherine Morin, "How the Ritz-Carlton Creates a 5 Star Customer Experience," CRM.org, December 13, 2019, pp. 1–12.

13. Micah Solomon, "Ritz-Carlton President Herve Humler's Leadership, Culture and Customer Service Secrets," *Forbes* (www.forbes.com), April 21, 2015, p. 9.

14. Suzanne J. Peterson, Benjamin M. Galvin, and Donald Lange, "CEO Servant Leadership: Exploring Executive Characteristics and Firm Performance," *Personnel Psychology*, Number 3, 2012, pp. 565–596.

15. Robert C. Liden, Sandy J. Wayne, Chenwei Liao, and Jeremy Meuser, "Servant Leadership and Serving Culture: Influence on Individual and Unit Performance," *Academy of Management Journal*, October 2014, pp. 1434–1452.

16. Emily M. Hunter, et al., "Servant Leaders Inspire Servant Followers: Antecedents and Outcomes for Employees and the Organization," *The Leadership Quarterly*, April 2013, pp. 316–331.

17. Fred O. Walumbwa, Chad A. Hartnell, and Adegoke Oke, "Servant Leadership, Procedural Justice Climate, Service Climate, Employee Attitudes, and Organizational Citizenship Behavior: A Cross-Level Investigation," *Journal of Applied Psychology*, May 2010, pp. 517–529.

18. Myriam Chiniara and Kaathleen Bentein, "Linking Servant Leadership to Individual Performance: Differentiating the Mediating Role of Autonomy, Competence and Relatedness Need Satisfaction," *The Leadership Quarterly*, February 2016, pp. 124–141.

19. Dan Cable, "How Humble leadership Really Works," *Harvard Business Review* (https://hbr.org), April 23, 2018, pp. 1–8; Josh Spiro, "How to Become a Servant Leader," *Inc.* (www.inc.com), pp. 1–8; "Lindsay," "9 Ways To Become a Better Servant Leader," *Leadership Inspirations* (https://leadershipinspirationscom), April 16, 2018, pp. 1–8; Melissa Maldonado, "10 Steps to Become a Servant Leader," *AUTO/ MATE* (www.automate.com), December 11, 2019, pp. 1–4; Dan Price, "Become a Servant Leader in 4 Steps," *Success*, January 25, 2017.

20. Original story based on the following sources: James R Hagerty, "Toro Head Promoted Servant Leadership," *The Wall Street Journal*, May 16–17, 2020, p. A11; Ben Lichtenwainer and Radian Forest, "Ken Melrose Completes His Service on Earth," *Modern Servant Leader* (www.modernservantleader.com), 2008–2020, pp. 1–3; Andy Goldstein, "Ken Melrose: Being a Difference, Then, and Now," *National Association of State Board of Accounting* (https://nasba.org), May 15, 2012, pp. 1–4; "An Interview with Ken Melrose, Toro Company's Former CEO," *Theology at Work Project* (www.theologyofwork.org), February 16, 2006, pp. 1–6.

8

Narcissism, Hubris, and Charisma Blended with Humility

A striking advantage of humility for leaders and professionals is that it can be used to soften the impact of strong and potentially overwhelming attributes of narcissism and hubris. Charisma is usually perceived as a more positive attribute than narcissism or hubris, yet a dose of humility can also enhance the effectiveness of charisma.

A case in point of the theme of this chapter is Victoria, an outstanding successful Realtor ®. She is the leading agent in her region. As a positive narcissist, Victoria has her photo included on the for-sale signs of houses she lists herself, and also on the signs of the members of the ten-person team she has assembled. On her website, Victoria writes that it takes a very special person (herself) to be totally sensitive to the needs and desires of a client. Victoria also describes how she has maintained a record of being number one in her region for many years,

In contact with clients, Victoria softens her narcissism with astute listening to understand her client's needs and concerns. Two of her most-asked questions are "How can my firm and I best serve you?" and "What would make this real-estate transaction an amazing success for you?"

THE CHARACTERISTICS OF A NARCISSISTIC LEADER

To better understand how a touch of humility can be woven into narcissism it is helpful to first dig into the nature of narcissism as it relates to leadership. *Narcissism* is a relatively stable personality trait characterized by a

DOI: 10.4324/9781003461784-8

sense of personal superiority, a desire for power, and an exaggerated sense of self-importance. The definition offered by the American Psychiatric Association is a little harsher contending that narcissism is a grandiose preoccupation with one's own self-importance. The narcissist believes that he or she is special and more important than others.[1] Most narcissists have little empathy for others because they are so focused on themselves. The accompanying self-quiz gives you the opportunity to think about your own level of narcissism, as well as pin-pointing the behaviors and attitudes of workplace narcissists.

THE NARCISSISM CHECKLIST

Listed below are 25 behaviors and attitudes experienced by people who have varying degrees of narcissism. Check "yes" whether each behavior or attitude that applies to you in the sense that you have acted or thought in such a manner. People who are highly narcissistic, however, often do not perceive their own behavior and attitudes accurately. If feasible, to verify the accuracy of your responses to the checklist, have a person who knows you well help you respond to the checklist.

Statement about Narcissism	Yes	No
1. Patronizes and criticizes others.		
2. Hates to be criticized.		
3. Strongly dislikes disagreements with others.		
4. Becomes quite upset when cannot control a conversation.		
5. Very little concern for others.		
6. Thinks first of self.		
7. Works hard at maintaining an inflated image of self.		
8. Thinks more about extraordinary achievements than carrying out daily responsibilities.		
9. Works hard to maintain a façade of wealth.		
10. Convinced of own superiority.		
11. Dependent on others for frequent doses of admiration and affection.		
12. Invests a disproportionate amount of personal income into clothing and other attire.		
13. Owns or leases a vehicle that he or she thinks will impress others with its luxury.		

Statement about Narcissism	Yes	No
14. Abuses and insults others without feeling the least bit guilty.		
15. Believes that he or she can accomplish anything with proper effort.		
16. Believes that he or she should receive special treatment because of wonderful personal qualities.		
17. Belies that other people are envious of him or her.		
18. Acts like a snob.		
19. Will often say something to the effect of "Oh, how nice" when someone else describes a personal accomplishment.		
20. Often bullies others.		
21. Intense envy about the accomplishments and possessions of others.		
22. Poor team player because of the need to be the center of attention.		
23. Frequently finds fault with other people and things.		
24. Quick to blame somebody else for his or her own mistake.		
25. Feels uncomfortable when another person receives praise and recognition in his or her presence.		

Scoring and Interpretation: The more of these behaviors and attitudes you have demonstrated or felt, the more your level of narcissism is creating problems for you in the workplace. If 15 or more of these behaviors and attitudes apply to you, you may have to take corrective action to become less of an annoyance to others so you can improve your interpersonal relations with work associates. Attaining work goals often requires collaboration, so if you decrease your narcissistic behaviors and attitudes, you will most likely be more productive.

As a personality trait, narcissism consists of both a general trait and sub-traits or components. The general trait of narcissism reflects the definition just presented, an extremely positive and inflated view of the self, combined with little empathy for others. Studies based on the Narcissistic Personality Inventory (similar to the self-quiz just presented) have revealed seven sub-traits, all of relevance to leadership and professional behavior.[2]

1. *Authority.* Authority refers to a person's leadership skills and power. People who score high on authority like to be in charge and gain power, often for power's sake alone. A person who scored high on authority would have the self-image of a leader, and would be someone who values power. A professional who scored high on authority would want to be looked up to for his or her knowledge by clients.

2. *Self-Sufficiency.* As implied in its label, self-sufficiency refers to how much a person relies on others versus his or her own abilities to meet his or her own needs in life. A person who scores high on self-sufficiency would behave independently, such as not frequently consulting others before taking action or making a decision. A humble leader typically behaves in the opposite way.

3. *Superiority.* This trait refers to whether a person feels he or she is superior to others in close contact. The higher the score the haughtier and more superior the person thinks he or she is in comparison to others. A humble leader or professional would of course score low on this meaning of superiority.

4. *Exhibitionism (not the sexual kind!).* Exhibitionism refers to a person's need to be the center of attention, and willingness to ensure that they are the center of attention, even at the expense of others. A person who scored high on exhibitionism might take up a subordinate's or client's time explaining how he or she was stranded in an airport for two days.

5. *Exploitation.* This trait refers to a person's willingness to exploit others in order to meet his or her own needs or goals. Exploiting could take many forms such as stealing ideas from others, asking a co-worker to do some of your work when you are overloaded, and borrowing money without repaying. A leader with a strong tendency toward exploitation might ask a group member to run personal errands for him or her.

6. *Vanity.* Vanity refers to a belief in one's own abilities and attractiveness compared to others, thereby fitting the usual definition of vain. A leader who scored high on the trait of vanity would typically think that his or her suggestions and creative ideas were superior to those from the group. Leaders with humility score low on the trait of vanity.

7. *Entitlement.* This trait refers to the amount of entitlement a person expects in life. In this context, entitlement refers to unreasonable expectations of especially favorable treatment or automatic compliance with one's expectations. People with a high standing on this trait generally have a greater expectation of entitlement whereas those who score lower expect little from others or from life.

A leader who possessed the traits just described to a high degree would rarely be humble. Yet a moderate standing on a few of these traits combined with humility could be a winning combination, as described in the next section.

An attitude of narcissistic leaders that can be added to this list of seven traits has been identified by leadership coach Lolly Daskal. She says that assuming you are the smartest person in the room can be a dangerous mindset. It can lead to insufficient open-mindedness and a tendency to dismiss the ideas and perspectives of subordinates, coworkers, superiors, and customers. Thinking that you are the smartest person in the room (a narcissistic quality) can hinder your leadership development because you become close-minded.[3]

THE NARCISSIST TINGED WITH HUMILITY

Most writing and observations about workplace narcissists indicate that they are a negative force in organizations. A major complaint is that the self-absorption of narcissists blocks them from being much help to others. A more realistic perception about narcissists in the workplace is that some of them are healthy and productive, despite the occasional chagrin they cause for others. With a reasonable dose of narcissism, a person can be productive in a high-level position. Many successful sales representatives, particularly those specializing in consumer products, are self-adoring and flamboyant. Yet their level of narcissism is not so high that it prevents them from empathizing with customers.

Many highly successful real-estate agents tend toward narcissism with some of them dressing in a top-of-the-line fashion. A large proportion of successful business leaders have sufficient narcissistic tendencies to be flamboyant and self-promoting, yet subordinates respond positively to their leadership. Many entrepreneurs tend toward being narcissistic because their love for the product or service they are promoting is intertwined with self-admiration.

According to Sigmund Freud, one of the reasons that a moderate degree of narcissism in adults can facilitate a person's being healthy and productive is that healthy narcissism is an essential part of normal development.[4] A moderate degree of narcissism might be the most effective because the person would most likely have enough self-esteem and extraversion to impress others and have good interpersonal relationships. When the trait of narcissism is too low, the person might have too many self-doubts and be too low in self-confidence to succeed. When the trait of narcissism is too high, the person suffers from problems such as being perceived as obnoxious and uninterested in the welfare of others.

The accompanying checklist might be helpful in thinking about how some of your attitudes and behaviors could be contributing to a positive or negative degree of narcissism.

A CHECKLIST OF POTENTIALLY POSITIVE ATTITUDES AND BEHAVIORS ASSOCIATED WITH NARCISSISM

Attitude or Behavior	Fits Me
1. I am quite proud of my appearance.	
2. I am quite proud of how I express myself.	
3. People are drawn to me at networking events.	
4. I smile frequently because I know that people appreciate it.	
5. I frequently compliment others so they will like me.	
6. I feel quite comfortable being photographed.	
7. I dress much more carefully than most people in my network.	
8. I am quite confident that I can successfully complete almost all assignments given to me.	
9. My mistakes are so few that I hardly use excuse-making.	
10. Negative feedback just gives me another suggestion for being more successful.	
11. When I receive a compliment, I conclude that the compliment giver has good judgment.	
12. I already own or plan to own vanity license plates.	

Attitude or Behavior	Fits Me
13. People who know me well think highly of my potential for promotion. 14. My talents are in demand. 15. I make a wonderful first impression.	

Scoring and Interpretation: If you believe that between 9 and 13 of these statements fit you well, it could be that you have a level of narcissism that is an asset in work and personal life in terms of establishing relationships with people. Yet if you believe that 14 or 15 of these statements fit you well your level of conceit and narcissism could create interpersonal friction. If you believe that only 8 or fewer of these statements fit you well, you might be expressing low self-confidence and low self-esteem.

A major contributor to narcissism being an asset for a leader or professional is a dose of humility. Bradley Owens and his colleagues argued that although the combination of humility and narcissism may appear paradoxical, in reality the traits can exist simultaneously. Furthermore, it is possible for narcissism and humility to work together harmoniously to result in leader effectiveness. Humility can facilitate narcissistic leaders being effective because the most self-focused toxic dimensions of narcissism are counteracted by a leader being humble.

The narcissistic tendencies toward exploring others, being self-absorbed, demanding admiration are offset by drawing attention to the strengths and contributions of others. A sense of superiority can be neutralized by a leader's admission of limitations and mistakes. Furthermore, an intense desire for personal success can be balanced with recognizing the desire of group members to also be successful. A strong desire to have authority over others can be countered by a willingness to grant others some authority based on their expertise in the task at hand.

To investigate whether it is true that a touch of humility can enhance the effectiveness of narcissistic leaders, Owen and his colleagues conducted a study in a large healthcare organization. The participants were 876 employees, 76 percent of whom were female, and 138 leaders,

61 percent of whom were female. The leaders responded to a self-quiz about narcissism, and direct reports rated their leaders with respect to humility. Measures were also taken of four leader outcomes: perceived leader effectiveness, employee job engagement, leader evaluations of employee job performance, and objective productivity data about employee performance. The three major findings of the study were as follows:

- Narcissistic leaders with high humility are perceived by followers as more effective than their counterparts with low humility.
- Narcissistic leaders with high humility have more engaged group members than their counterparts with low humility.
- Narcissistic leaders with high humility have higher-performing group members than their counterparts with low humility.

A key practical implication of the study was that narcissistic leaders who display some humble behavior may help to prevent their narcissism from damaging their leadership effectiveness. Leader narcissism can have a positive effect on the perception and motivation of direct reports when it is tempered by humility.[5]

The importance of narcissistic leaders remembering to display humility while interacting with followers can be inferred from a study conducted in the Netherlands. The setting for the study was a large retail organization, with 175 store leaders and 555 non-leaders responding to questionnaires. A major finding of the study was that the more opportunities followers have to observe narcissistic leaders, the more they will experience these leaders' toxic behaviors, such as exploiting people. Narcissistic leaders who were more visible, and therefore seen more frequently by group members, were therefore perceived to be less effective. When store associates had fewer opportunities to observe their leader, the results were quite different. Leader narcissism was positively related to perceived leader effectiveness and attitudes about the job.[6]

The message from this study related to leader humility and narcissism is a little convoluted. "Visibility" or being physically present is a productive leadership behavior. Yet when a narcissistic leader has substantial visibility, he or she is likely to be perceived as less effective. The way out of this bind for the narcissistic leader is to consciously practice humility when physically present (or using meeting technology).

THE SERVANT LEADER WITH A TINGE OF NARCISSISM

A servant leader is generally thought to be the polar opposite of a narcissistic leader. The servant leader looks for ways to be helpful to others, to serve them, and to be concerned primarily about the welfare of constituents. Servant leaders promote the interests of others over and above self-interest. A paradox, however, is that a tinge of narcissism, or at least self-interest, might strengthen the servant leader's effectiveness. The expression of self-interest might help the servant leader avoid the image of being too weak and servile. Here are a handful of possibilities of how a servant leader might enter a tinge of narcissism to enhance his or her effectiveness:

- The servant leader product manager might say to the group, "My job is to do what I can to help you make this product launch successful. And quite frankly it would make me feel good to be associated with a great product launch."
- The servant leader CMO (chief marketing officer) might say to the group, "I have listened to all your suggestions on how we can grab a bigger market share, and I am impressed. Based on my 15 years of experience in the field, I would like to build a little on your suggestions and present a different idea."
- The servant leader head of industrial engineering might say to a junior member of the department, "Part of my role is to help you develop and succeed as an industrial engineer. Yet I cannot be much help if you ignore most of my best ideas designed to help you."
- The servant leader manager of a fulfillment center might announce to a group of frontline workers, "I know that we are experiencing an unprecedented surge in orders. I am going to spend 30 hours this week along with you packing boxes for shipment. But you have to keep in mind that next week I must return to my own work in planning and preparing budgets."
- The servant leader COO (chief operations manager) explains to his management team during a downsizing, "I want to delegate as much as possible to you folks. Yet during a downsizing, I must personally approve the list of people to be downsized."

HUBRIS COMBINED WITH A TOUCH OF HUMILITY

Hubris is closely related to narcissism because *hubris* is an exaggerated sense of self-confidence. Research has suggested that CEOs with hubris have a tendency to make risky acquisition and investment decisions.[7] Contrary to traditional either-or-thinking, it is possible for people to have hubris and some humility simultaneously. When the founder of Intel, Robert Noyce, was asked how he felt about being known as the "Father of Silicon Valley," his response was "You know it makes me a little bit proud, and a little bit humble." Noyce illustrated the sweet spot between hubris and humility that can be a contributor to major success. He had the chutzpah to believe that he could really change the world, but also seemed to realize that he was but a microscopic speck in the universe, and expressed humility about his contributions.[8]

Scott Miller of the Franklin Covey Institute offers two relevant ideas about balancing humility and hubris. One suggestion is to lift others along the way. If you earn a leadership role, others will be denied that position and feel dejected, passed over, and perhaps envious. Do not ignore or minimize these feelings. As you are climbing the hierarchy, throw a rope down and lift the other people with you (an act of humility). Encourage those envious people to climb above you. If you are confident of both your character and competence (at least a touch of hubris), your shoulder can handle some weight.

A second relevant idea is to dance with the people who helped you get promoted. You most likely did not earn your leadership position all on your own. Most likely many people coached you, taught you, were patient toward you, and were confident in your abilities. Instead of abandoning these people, display loyalty to those who believed in you and will continue to be your confidantes and sounding boards.[9]

THE COMBINATION OF CHARISMA AND HUMILITY

The term *charisma* is often used loosely to apply to any individual with a warm smile and positive personality. Used more precisely in reference to leadership, charisma is the ability to lead others based on personal charm, magnetism, inspiration, and emotion. Charismatic leaders and professionals are usually outgoing, self-confident, and frequently draw attention to themselves. Many charismatic leaders are also narcissistic. The narcissistic leader can be charming except when engaging in excessive self-puffery and blaming others for mistakes. Despite these potential negative behaviors, charismatic leaders can show humility.

A starting point in understanding how charismatic leaders can be humble, is to recognize how some charismatic leaders use their power. A socialized charismatic leader uses power to benefit others. This type of leader also attempts to bring group members' values in line with his or her values. The socialized charismatic formulates and pursues goals that fulfill the needs of group members and provide intellectual stimulation to them. He or she usually has an interest in the welfare of constituents.

Followers of socialized charismatics are autonomous, empowered, and responsible. A study conducted in a healthcare organization indicated that direct reports of leaders perceived to be socialized charismatics are less likely to engage in workplace deviance (such as lying, stealing, and cheating). Part of the reason is that the socialized charismatic imparts positive values to group members. A socialized charismatic therefore functions as a servant (and humble) leader.

The effect of the socialized charismatic on followers provides more insight into this type of charismatic. In a socialized relationship, the followers have a clear sense of who they are and a clear set of values. The charismatic relationship gives them an opportunity to express their important values within the framework of being a group member, such as wanting to work together to preserve the planet. (The opportunity for group members to express their values is characteristic of humble leadership.) In a socialized relationship, the followers derive a sense of direction and self-expression not from identifying with the leader but from the leader's message.[10] The message of the socialized charismatic in this situation might be, "We want to make money but we want to contribute to a sustainable environment at the same time."

In contrast to the charismatic leader with humility is the personalized charismatic. Such individuals serve primarily their own interests and so exercise few restraints on their use of power. Personalized charismatics impose self-serving goals on constituents, and they offer consideration and support to group members only when it facilitates their own goals.

Followers of personalized charismatics are typically obedient, submissive, and dependent.[11] They also identify more with the leader than the leader's message and therefore might follow the leader down an unethical path, such as granting homeowner loans that will most likely result in a high foreclosure rate.

The potential humility component of charismatic leaders can also be understood by examining how being humble can be included in a few of their notable characteristics. In other words, there is little room to blend humility into a few of the bold characteristics of charismatic leaders.

A key characteristic of charismatic leaders is their vision. They offer a vision (lofty goal) of where the organization is headed and how it can get there (a plan). A vision is multifaceted, extending beyond the organization's present goals. A sense of vision inspires employees to perform well. With a touch of humility, charismatic leaders often use input from workers to craft their visions so that the vision will appear more realistic. Part of being humble is to minimize grandiosity. The vision of technology firm Starfire Systems suggests a realistic rather than a grandiose vision:

> *Starfire Systems will pioneer the creation of new advanced materials through enabling technology based on a wide range of ceramic forming polymers that meet the needs of customers.*

Charismatic leaders are masterful communicators. They formulate believable dreams and portray their vision of the future as the only path to follow. Charismatics also use metaphors to inspire people. An example is a favorite aphorism of Richard Marcus, the president of Neiman-Marcus stores: "If you follow in someone else's footsteps, you never get ahead." To be humble, the charismatic leader with strong communication skills might intersperse questions into his or her conversation with constituents, such as:

- "What holes do you see in my vision?"
- "What is your reaction to my ideas for increasing revenue this quarter?"
- "To implement my suggestions what help would you need from me?"

Almost by definition, leaders perceived as charismatic by group members have high standing on the trait of extraversion. Quite often leaders as well as others are labeled as charismatic because they are friendly and outgoing. The charismatic leader can add a touch of humility to extraversion by consciously reverting to introversion from time to time. For example, during a physical or virtual meeting, the leader can remain silent for a while to encourage others to participate.

Charismatic leaders at their best inspire trust, and a touch of humility is a trust builder.

Quite often their followers are willing to gamble their careers to follow their chief's vision such as accepting a low starting salary with stock opinions based on the startup's vision of great success.

Charismatic leaders are adept at managing their impression well which helps them to be perceived as charismatic. Impression management can take place at the physical level, such as an appealing appearance, yet can also take place at an intellectual level. An intellectual example would be a person indicating that he or she has powerful contacts, such as by saying, "Elon Musk and I were just discussing the future of driverless cars last week." A skilled charismatic might add a self-effacing comment to soften the impression management. In relation to the two examples just given, here are matching self-effacing comments:

- "Thanks for the compliment about my sweater. I love the sweater selection at Walmart."
- "Of course, Musk wouldn't talk to me unless he was convinced that I could afford a Tesla."

Charismatic leaders are often at the center of networks for giving and receiving advice which helps them to be perceived as charismatic, and this perception has been shown to enhance team performance.[12] The study that reached this conclusion measured in-person interactions, yet social media networks might attain the same result. Being at the center of an advice network is a robust opportunity for the charismatic leader to display humility. Asking others for their opinion and for advice is a hallmark characteristic of a humble leader. At the same time, charismatic professionals in the network can demonstrate humility by asking others for advice and opinions,

A CHARISMATIC AND HUMBLE LEADER: MARY BARRA, CEO OF GM

Mary Barra is Chairman and Chief Executive Officer of General Motors Company, a dual title she has held since January 2016, and has served as CEO since January 2015. Departing CEO Dan Akerson stated that he picked Barra to be his successor based on her ability to "make order out of chaos." Even during turbulent times such as during the job cuts and plant closings in 2019, GM employees perceived Barra to be a charismatic and passionate leader. She is at her best when she is in meetings or conversations with employees.

Leadership writer Steven Snyder has described Barra as humble and collaborative, eager to give credit to her team rather than seeking the spotlight for herself. She also exudes a sense of quiet self-confidence that prompts people to trust and admire her. Barra believes in continuous learning for herself as well as others. She took time away from her busy position to attend a Harvard Business School program. In each of her roles previous to becoming CEO, Barra learned crucial new skills, including global finance, marketing, and sales, Snyder also credits Barra with coming across as a genuine, caring, and authentic human being.

Barra has practiced the hands-on style of leadership characteristic of many leaders with humility. She told a reporter for *The Michigan Daily*,

> *I try to make sure that I understand the key parts of a business, and having worked in an assembly plant, having been a plant manager, having been responsible for product development, having understood HR, really round out to give me a lot of the skills I need as a CEO.*

Barra emphasized also that she has been involved in the physical process of creating a vehicle.

Under Barra's leadership the company has focused on strengthening its core business of manufacturing cars, trucks, and crossovers. At the same time GM has strived to lead the transformation of personality mobility through advanced technologies such as connectivity, autonomous driving, and vehicle sharing. In referring to the changes in the automobile industry, Barra said, "In this area of rapid transformation, you have to have a culture that's agile. We still have a lot of work to do."

Previous to her appointment as head of product development in 2011, Barra spent four years as Vice President of Global Human Resources. Joining GM after graduation as an electrical engineer, she was soon identified as a person with executive potential. She moved up the corporate ladder steadily in jobs in manufacturing, administration, and internal communications before the HR position. As the CEO, Barra was expected to change the culture of a company for which she had worked her entire career.

The GM board regards Barra as one of his key change agents in his efforts to remake the company culture that was often slow-moving. The company has long been known for the "GM nod," or agreeing to do something in a meeting, and then forgetting the issue. The CEO before Barra identified her as "a strong leader and change agent who knows the business inside and out."

In one of her initiatives to change the culture, Barra has helped GM loosen the controls over engineers, allowing them more creative freedom with vehicles. She said her approach is "empowering them to make the decisions, and I think you see it with some of the vehicles we just put out, whether it's the Chevrolet Impala or the Cadillac CTS or the Corvette."

Barra has long shown a humanistic touch during her leadership career at GM. When asked why she reduced the company's dress code from ten pages to "dress appropriately" while she was the head of human resources, Barra said,

> It really becomes a window into the change that we needed to make at General Motors. I can trust you with $10 million of budget and supervising 20 people, but I can't trust you to dress appropriately. It was kind of a step [forward] in empowerment. This really encouraged people to step up.

Barr prefers not to directly oppose or disagree with her managers. Instead, she channels everyone's energy by empowering them to make relatively obvious decisions for themselves. She says she wants them to "take ownership of the rules and understand that they are accountable to lead their own team." Business writer Bob Rosen observes that from a human perspective, Barra amplifies and directs her people's energy by being a model of authenticity, courage, integrity, and resilience.

Barra believes that her thrust for creative freedom and simplicity will strengthen GM in the long term. She is adamant about leading by persuasion rather than direct commands. Barra said that when employees say "I'm doing it because Mary told me to do it" is the day she loses. Barra recognizes that culture change only takes place when people change their behavior, such as taking more responsibility for problems.

Even before becoming CEO, Barra was remarkably candid with and honest with staff members. While head of product development, her primary directive to engineers and designers was, "No more crappy cars." She thought that too many boundaries were placed on employees that did not give them a recipe for success. "So now we're saying no excuses," Barra said. "If it's a budget, if it's resources, we have to do great cars, trucks, and crossovers and it's our job to enable you to do that."

In return for her candor, Barra asks for frankness in return. She respects the opinion of GM employees and wants them to speak up when something is wrong, and to confront problems directly. Barra uses social media extensively to connect with GM staffers.

When describing her leadership approach. Barra hints about her humility. She says that most people want their leaders to be authentic, and to have integrity. Workers want to have meaningful conversations and to be approached with empathy, fairness, and respect. When concerns are raised, the leader should not say, "No you are wrong," or "I disagree." Barra thinks a better approach is to respond with a question or comment that emphasizes your shared concern but does not place the other person in a defensive position. She believes that if you are willing to address others in a problem-solving manner when there is confusion about a course of action, then you will experience more collaboration and positive energy.

Barra displays humility in another subtle way. She does not deny that GM encounters problems, but instead is willing to make tough decisions to find a solution. In 2023 GM announced a buyout program as part of an initiative to reduce costs by $2 billion by the end of 2024 to help finance the manufacture of electric vehicles. The buyout program involved 5,000 white-collar employees, and was aimed at preventing another layoff. In February of 2023, GM laid off 500 of the company's 167,000 employees to reduce costs.

Barra received a bachelor of science in electrical engineering (BSEE) from the General Motors Institute (now Kettering University). Later she graduated with an MBA from Stanford University. She was raised in a GM family, with her father having been a die-maker in a Pontiac plant for 39 years.[13]

GUIDELINES FOR ACTION

1. A touch of humility can be effective in softening the impact of narcissism and hubris.

2. A person with narcissistic tendencies has to work extra hard at developing empathy for others because a natural tendency for a narcissist is to lack empathy.

3. If you work for a narcissistic boss or with a narcissistic co-worker, be on guard about having your best ideas stolen.

4. A strong sense of entitlement works against being humble because you expect so much from other people.

5. A workplace narcissist can be healthy and productive, particularly when the narcissism is sprinkled with a touch of humility.

6. A moderate degree of narcissism is usually the best for a leader or professional because the person would most likely have enough self-esteem and extraversion to impress others and have good interpersonal relationships.

7. A major contributor to narcissism being an asset for a leader or professional is a dose of humility. It is possible for narcissism and humility to work together harmoniously to result in leadership effectiveness.

8. Narcissistic leaders who display some humble behavior may help to prevent their narcissism from damaging their leadership effectiveness.

9. A tinge of narcissism, or at least self-interest, might help the servant leader avoid the image of being too weak and servile.

10. Contrary to traditional either-or thinking, it is possible for people to have hubris and some humility simultaneously.

11. One way of balancing humility and hubris is to lift others as you succeed in a leadership position.

12. If as a charismatic leader you use power in order to benefit others, you are functioning as a servant (and humble) leader.

13. With a touch of humility, charismatic leaders can use input from workers to craft their visions so that the vision will appear more realistic.

14. Charismatic leaders at their best inspire trust, and a touch of humility is a trust builder.
15. Being at the center of an advice network is a robust opportunity for the charismatic leader to display humility because he or she can ask for opinions and advice.

NOTES

1. American Psychiatric Association, *Diagnostic and Statistical Manual of Mental Disorders*, 5th edition (Arlington, VA: American Psychiatric Association, 2013).
2. Robert Raskin and C. S. Hall, "A Narcissistic Personality Inventory," *Psychological Reports*, Volume 44, 1979, p. 590.
3. Lolly Daskal, "What's Holding You Back in Your Leadership Development?" www .lollydaskal.com, copyright© 1991–2023, p. 1.
4. Sigmund Freud, "On Narcissism." In J. Strachey (Editor), *The Standard Edition of the Complete Works of Sigmund Freud* (London: Hogarth Press 1957), Volume 14, pp. 69–102 Original work published in 1914.
5. Bradley P. Owens, Angela S. Wallace, and David A. Waldman, "Leader Narcissism and Follower Outcomes: The Counterbalancing Effect of Leader Humility," *Journal of Applied Psychology*, July 2015, pp. 1203–1213.
6. Barbara Nevicka et al, "Narcissistic Leaders: An Asset or Liability? Leader Visibility, Follower Responses, and Group-Level Absenteeism," *Journal of Applied Psychology*, July 2018, pp. 703–723.
7. Julian Barling, "The Science of Leadership: Lessons from Research for Organizational Leaders" (New York: Oxford University Press, 2014), p. 51.
8. Christopher Bergland, "The Sweet Spot Between Hubris and Humility: Greatness Lies in Balancing Self-Belief with Egolessness," March 3, 2013, p. 1.
9. Scott Miller, "Balancing Humility and Hubris," *FranklinCovey* (https://resources .franklincovey.com) ©2018, pp. 1–6.
10. Michael E. Brown and Linda K. Treviño, "Leader-Follower Values Congruence: Are Socialized Charismatic Leaders Better Able to Achieve It?" *Journal of Applied Psychology*, March 2009, pp. 478–490.
11. Jane M. Howell and Boss Shamir, "The Role of Followers in the Charismatic Leadership Process: Relationships and Their Consequences," *Academy of Management Review*, January 2005, p. 100.
12. Prasad Balkundi, Martin Kilduff, and David A. Harrison, "Centrality and Charisma: Conquering How Leader Networks and Attributions Affect Team Performance," *Journal of Applied Psychology*, November 2011, pp. 1209–1222.
13. Original story based on facts and observations in the following sources: Serina Jiang, "General Motors CEO Mary Barra Shares Her Leadership Journey, Visions for the Future," *The Michigan Daily* (www.michigandaily.com), April 13, 2022,

pp. 1–6; Sadan Bin Sattar, "Leadership Qualities—Styles Traits, and Skills of May, Barra," *The Strategy Watch* (www.thestrategywatch.com), 2023, pp. 1–5; "Mary T Barra: Chairman and Chief Executive Officer, General Motors Company," *General Motors* (www.gm.com), July 2020, p. 1; Michael Wayland, "Barra Takes Her Case to the Factory Floor," *Automotive News* (www.automotivenews.com), February 25, 2019, pp. 1–4; Brian Bushard, "5,000 GM Employees Take Buyouts in Cost-Cutting Program," *Forbes* (www.forbes.com), April 4, 2023, pp. 1–3; Steve Snyder, "Five Leadership Lessons from General Motors CEO, Mary Barra," *Snyder Leadership* (www.snyderleadership.com) © 2020, pp. 1–3.

9

Developing and Enhancing Your Humility

Many readers of this book are probably wondering if humility can be developed, or if leaders and professionals who are already humble can enhance and hone this valuable trait and behavior. We believe strongly that with more knowledge about the subject, and the self-discipline to apply the knowledge, most people can make more effective use of humility. As humility researcher Michael Johnson of the University of Washington Foster School of Business notes, patience is a virtue, and some people are naturally more patient than others. "Humility is the same way. If we focus on appreciating the strengths of others, focus on being teachable, have an accurate view of ourselves, we can actually become more humble."[1]

In this chapter we look at many additional ways of developing and enhancing humility. These actions and attitudes are divided into those directed to yourself versus those directed toward other people. The emphasis is on self-development but executive or leadership coaching can be a useful intervention for developing and enhancing humility. Yet, for the results of coaching to last longer than a one-time spurt change toward more effective humility, the person would still have to apply self-disciplined practice to attain lasting change.

ACTIONS AND ATTITUDES DIRECTED TOWARD YOURSELF

A major part of acquiring, developing, or enhancing humility involves attitudes and actions directed toward yourself, including your self-perceptions.

DOI: 10.4324/9781003461784-9

Many of these actions and attitudes have been suggested by such topics as the components of humility, and the practices of humble leaders and professionals described in previous chapters.

Develop Passionate Curiosity

If you develop a hunger to learn, it helps make you humble because it helps you understand that there is so much relevant knowledge in the outside world that you do not already possess.[2] A reflex response of "so what" when you are exposed to new information that could be job-relevant strengthens smugness. The underlying premise of a so-what attitude is that you have enough knowledge to perform superbly in your role.

Being passionately curious helps you overcome another enemy of humility, the *confirmatory bias*. Humans are wired to selectively process only information that confirms what we know, and to selectively filter out information that contradicts what we know to be correct.[3] If you only accept information that confirms your present beliefs, you will continue to feel confident that you do not need new information—a very unhumble belief.

Roger, the marketing manager for heavy luxury motorcycles, believes that the new generation of bike riders highly value these beautiful machines from the past. He believes that with a little more advertising in the right media young motorcycle drivers will flock to the showroom to purchase luxury bikes. Yet most industry data suggest that the new generation of bikers want more nimble, lighter, and less expensive motorcycles. To support his opinion Roger takes seriously only a scattering of reports suggesting young drivers are ready for big bikes. He ignores contradictory information.

To help become passionately curious and overcome the confirmatory bias at the same time, it is helpful to frequently ask yourself, "What information could I possibly use to be more effective in my role?" or "What evidence exists that I could possibly be wrong in my assumption?"

Admit What You Do Not Know

Admitting that you do not know something is a basic characteristic of a humble person. Humble leaders are comfortable in telling group members that they do not have all the answers. They are able to say, "I don't know the answer or the exact course of action to take, but I will find out." Leaders with humility are also comfortable inviting the input of others, with a statement such as "I don't know. What do you feel is the best solution?"[4]

It is not easy for many people to admit what they do not know, but it is helpful to flash a cautionary signal to yourself when appropriate. Say to yourself something like, "Watch out not to bluff here. I will come across as ineffective if I say I know how to use algorithms to select employees who are likely to stay with the firm three years or more."

Related to admitting that you do not know something, is the fear of making mistakes and bruising our egos. We sometimes play it safe to avoid looking ill-informed or fail in front of work associates. Edward Hess, a professor at the Darden Graduate School of Business at the University of Virginia, says that being okay with being wrong is a necessary and important part of developing humility. He asserts, "To proceed more fearlessly into the future, you need to understand that learning is not an efficient 99 percent defect-free process—so mistakes have to be valued as learning opportunities."[5]

The opportunity to develop humility here is that making an occasional mistake does not make you look bad, and will often be interpreted as you being courageous enough to try something new. After making an acquisition that failed, a CEO might say to her management team,

We paid $10 million for that startup that we thought would fill a hole in our product line. The company proved to be a dud, and we sold it for $7 million yesterday. I am sorry that I wasted company resources, but I think I know where our due diligence went wrong.

Believe in Something Bigger than Yourself

You may recall that leaders with humility are transcendent, in the sense that they believe something outside themselves is more important than they are. At the center of the lives of humble leaders is a value system that drives their beliefs and action.[6] These leaders think that there is something in the external world more important than themselves. The external cause could be a religious belief, or a value that extends beyond the self. Identifying something bigger than yourself that your leadership or professional efforts are pursuing might require careful introspection. A team leader at a manufacturer of tires for vehicles might reflect, "What we are doing here is bigger than me or my team. By manufacturing long-lasting, high-quality tires we help people have a safer work and personal life. We are also preventing thousands of accidents and deaths."

Another example of something bigger than yourself to believe in would be faith in science. A leader might think that the laboratory group he or she manages is contributing to the advancement of science, and that science uncovers the truth and betters humankind.

Be a Model of Humility for Others

Research was cited in previous chapters that a servant leader establishes a model for service that is emulated by many employees. If you model what you want others to do you are both humble and perceived as humble. Journalist Quint Studer suggests that to be humble never ask your team to do anything you are not willing to do, or expect them to maintain standards you are unable or willing to keep.[7] The origin of the idea of not expecting the group to do something you would not do seems to be in the days when supervisors were chosen because they were the most skilled group members. In reality, today's leaders cannot perform all the group tasks, such as the production supervisor being able to program a robot.

Yet to enhance your humility, it is worth jumping in and performing tasks that you can do such as a customer support manager dealing with an intensely angry customer. Or a restaurant manager might fill in for a server who was absent for the day.

Use Mistakes and Setbacks to Keep You Humble

An easy way to feel humble is to reflect on mistakes and setbacks you have experienced. If you share these experiences with group members you will be perceived as humble. Leadership development specialist Russ L. Moxley points out that humility is a lesson learned from mistakes. Mistakes often inform people about their flaws and limitations. One executive told Moxley the story of how he did a poor job of negotiating a contract with a major international client that cost the company thousands of dollars. The executive said, "I didn't ask for help. I didn't think I needed it. I learned very quickly how much I didn't know. I learned it the hard way."[8]

Former heavyweight champion Mike Tyson, who in 2024 fought at age 58, is noted as having said: "Everybody has a plan until they get punched in the mouth." According to leadership coach Bill Treasurer, sharp and painful setbacks can rattle your self-confidence, often provoking the thought of withdrawing from the leadership ranks. But these moments can also inspire *transformative humiliation*, in which pain and embarrassment trigger positive changes that result in the leader becoming more grounded, authentic, and more effective. "It is precisely when you get humbled that you become humbler," says Treasurer.[9]

Learning from your mistakes is standard advice, but the humility aspect is particularly relevant here. Being set back or defeated helps a person recognize that he or she has room for improvement that translates into humility. A frequent example is the person who is bypassed for promotion with the explanation given that he or she is perceived as too aggressive and overbearing. If this message sinks in the bypassed person might be motivated to be humbler in dealing with work associates.

Understand Your Limitations

A key component of humility is to understand your limitations and weaknesses. It therefore follows logically that by carefully identifying your limitations you will become a humble leader or professional. (Later in this chapter we will describe the role of feedback from others in identifying your limitations.) Humble leaders are secure enough to recognize their weaknesses and to seek the input and talents of others. Rather than feel threatened, they surround themselves with people whose skill sets complement their own areas of weakness.[10]

It takes hard work to understand your limitations and to use this information to come across to others as demonstrating humility and to actually be humble. Take the example of Sam, the owner of a business with over 300 employees. To grow the business, Sam knows that he has to hire a handful of new talent. He then carefully reflects,

A major reason we do not have the right talent in a few key spots is that I have hired the wrong people. I am too easily fooled by a person who speaks a good game, and has a warm smile. I hire that person, and soon he or she proves to be a dud. I am going to ask my head of administration to help me with hiring key people. Or perhaps I will also get the help of a HR consulting firm. I won't let my blind spots in hiring people hold back our growth any longer.

Consider Yourself to Be a Steward

A self-image for a leader that fosters humility is to think of oneself as a steward rather than a powerful ruler. As a consultant with the Ken Blanchard Companies reminds us, unless you are the founder and owner of the business, you have been hired to manage and develop the entity that has been entrusted to you. Stewards understand that what they are responsible for is loaned to them and can be taken back quickly. A steward CEO, much like a servant leader, views his or her leadership as a responsibility to take care of, and nurture and grow the organization and its people.[11] Acting like a steward brings you humility because you recognize that your power is limited and that you are a caretaker.

Hold Yourself Accountable When Something Goes Wrong under Your Watch

A self-centered leader will frequently shift blame when something goes wrong under his or her command. For example, a self-centered HR manager whose company is not attaining its diversity goals might blame the shortfall on the biases and prejudices of hiring managers throughout the company. In contrast, a leader with humility holds himself or herself accountable for whatever goes wrong under his or her command.

Business writer Jess Johnson says that the most important tenet of being humble is owning up to your mistakes. When leaders accept responsibility for negative results, an atmosphere is fostered in which blaming and finger-pointing is minimized. Humble leaders can therefore serve as role models by encouraging accountability starting with themselves.[12]

Confront Your Negative Stereotypes and Prejudices. A person with humility minimizes negative stereotypes and prejudices because holding such beliefs implies that the person thinks he or she is fundamentally superior to another person or group. If you recognize and confront your negative stereotypes and prejudices, they can be controlled enough to avoid acting superior to others. Much less harm is done with positive stereotypes in the workplace. I remember talking with Todd, the owner of a construction company. He mentioned that he was looking to hire a few Mexican-American workers. When I asked him why this particular ethnic group, Todd replied, "Mexican-Americans have the best work ethic." You could argue, however, that Todd might be excluding some fine people from other ethical and racial groups in his quest to fill positions.

Negative stereotypes and prejudices can block humility by making the leader or professional appear condescending and patronizing toward another individual or group. An example would be an elementary school principal who thinks that only women can be effective as elementary school teachers. She therefore acts in a condescending manner toward male teachers at the school, with an occasional comment such as, "Nothing personal here Nate, but most of the parents of our children would prefer that their children have a woman teacher."

A plausible starting point in confronting negative stereotypes and prejudices is to write a list of at least ten ethnic, racial, age, sex, and political groups. Next make several candid, unfiltered, and unvarnished comments about each group. Look for instances of strong negativity because being aware of these attitudes might help you control them in interactions with work associates.

Engage in Self-Deprecating Humor

Humble people make ample use of self-deprecating humor. Yet, extensive humor of this type might suggest low self-esteem. It is therefore best to use a sprinkling of self-deprecating humor to develop your humility. Poking fun at yourself in a good-natured way helps build relationships with subordinates, co-workers, superiors, and customers. It requires sensitivity to know what self-deprecating comment might fit the occasion and therefore contribute to an image of moderate humility. Here are a couple of positive examples:

- Darwin, the CEO and founder of a drug research company, explains to his management team that he will be making a presentation to investors to raise more capital for the firm. He says to the group, "The fact that we have not shown a profit in three years under my command could be a distraction."
- Kelsey, the manager of the accounts payable department is being considered for promotion to the position of VP of finance. She says to the top management team, "I hope you won't hold it against me that I struggle to balance my checkbook each month."

Reflect on Your Contribution to a Problem or Conflict

A subtle way of demonstrating humility is to recognize how you might be contributing to conflict with another person. Assume that a subordinate or co-worker constantly disagrees with you or irritates you because of what you perceive to be negative personality characteristics. The unhumble person immediately assumes that all the fault lies with the person with whom he or she is in conflict. You can enhance your humility by carefully analyzing your contribution to the negative relationship between you and the other person. Ask yourself questions such as the following:

- Could it be that I am trying too hard to control this person?
- Do I send out negative facial expressions when interacting with this person?
- Could it be that I consider this person to be a rival for my position?
- Does this person remind me of somebody I disliked in the past?

Finding answers to questions of the above type might prompt you to approach the other individual in a more accepting, humble manner.

ACTIONS AND ATTITUDES DIRECTED TOWARD OTHERS

Although the distinction between actions and attitudes directed toward yourself versus others is not always clear cut, in this section we emphasize how to develop and enhance your humility through your interaction with others.

Obtain Feedback from Many Sources

The most systematic way of developing and enhancing humility is to obtain feedback from a variety of sources, even though your ego might be bruised and deflated from time to time. Feedback is the mechanism that tells the leader how he or she is doing, whether positive, negative or mediocre. Overwhelmingly positive feedback will obviously not contribute to your humility but consistent feedback about areas for improvement and weaknesses could make you humbler. *Consistent* is emphasized because one random negative comment should not be taken seriously because almost every leader or professional will be disliked by somebody. A useful rule of thumb is that you receive the same negative feedback from three different sources, the negative commentary is probably valid.

Leaders receive feedback both formally and informally. A primary source of formal feedback is a performance review or evaluation. If the leader's boss makes negative comments about the leader's behavior or performance, those comments could be a force toward becoming humbler. One of many examples of a humbling statement in a performance review would be, "You haven't contributed a creative idea in a long time."

Another widely used method of formal feedback is the 360-degree-feedback questionnaire. Subordinates complete the questionnaire, yet input is sometimes included also from superiors, co-workers, customers, suppliers, and even the leader himself or herself. The most useful 360-degree surveys also include space for write-in comments. Feedback sources are anonymous except for the possible self-input. Humility is fostered when the leader sees a few suggestions for improvement that touch on the same theme. Two examples: "Brittany is so rude to lower-ranking employees," and "Julio takes so long to make a decision."

Feedback useful in developing humility also stems from the spontaneous comments of people who work with the leader about his or her behavior and performance. A direct report, for example, might say, "Ted, I wish you would give me clearer instructions. I need more direction." For people to be willing to offer spontaneous feedback, the leader needs to create an environment whereby spontaneous feedback is encouraged and welcomed.

To enhance humility by receiving useful feedback, it is helpful to constructively ask, "How am I doing?" "What should I keep doing?" "What should I keep doing?" It is also helpful for the leader to ask specific questions about performance, such as "How could I have improved our Zoom meeting yesterday?"[13]

CEO coach Sabina Nawaz recommends that leaders should ask questions that require specific answers. During an informal conversation about how you are doing, ask for feedback that elicits specific information to generalized responses. Instead of asking "Do you have feedback for me?" Try something to the effect, "What did you notice about how well people at the meeting understood what I was saying about changing our strategy?" "What is one thing I should do more of or change?"[14]

Obtain Input before Making a Major Decision

Leaders with humility go light on making major decisions without input from others suggesting that an effective way of developing humility is to obtain such input. Gathering the input enhances the perception of the leader as having enough humility to recognize the usefulness of ideas from the group. The humblest approach would be to open the topic of what needs to be decided, and then let the group decide. This approach has been referred to as *democratic* decision-making. For many leaders, this would constitute so much humility, that others would think they are abdicating their role.

A light form of humility in decision-making is the *consultative* type in which the leader merely consults with the group before making a decision. Midway between the two extremes is *consensus* decision-making in which the leader shares the major problem with group members. Together they generate and evaluate alternatives and attempt to reach an agreement on a solution. Consensus is achieved when every member of the group feels that they have been consulted and their voices heard even if not everyone agrees that the decision is optimal.

Whether you use a consultative, democratic, or consensus decision-making style for making major decisions, it enhances your humility. Instead of relying solely on your own resources, you have worked collaboratively with the group.

Be Open and Transparent

Openness and transparency contribute to humility providing the person is not brutally candid and insulting. The reason is that sharing your thoughts helps avoid the image of being secretive and plotting. A humble CEO might say to employees during a town hall meeting, "We will have to work very hard this year to be profitable. If we are not profitable, we will not be able to afford year-end bonuses. That includes one for me." A CEO with limited humility is likely to be less revealing about year-end bonuses, and surprise workers with the bad news at the very end of the fiscal year.

Another aspect of openness and transparency is to explain what you are doing about a problem and admit that the plan may not work as well as you want. In the situation with the first CEO just mentioned, he might have added,

The management team has looked for ways to increase profits this year such as finding a few lower-price suppliers, and not replacing several of our associates who have quit. Fortunately, we haven't laid anybody off. Yet I cannot guarantee that the measures we have taken will improve profits for sure. We still have a revenue shortfall.

Develop Empathy

Finding ways to improve your empathy is a natural way of enhancing your humility. A relatively painless way to improve your empathy is to make the effort to ask people questions about what they want, how they see things, or how they feel about a work-related matter. Arthur Blank, the co-founder of Home Depot, offers a stellar example. He said that when he was running Home Depot, he would regularly stop the customers who walked out of Home Depot stores with no packages or bags in their arms. Somehow Home Depot had let them down. "Wrong stuff, wrong price, bad service—something," said Blank. "They would tell us what the issue was, and then we would just go in and fix the problem."

Blank took the same approach after buying the Atlanta Falcons football team. At the time 40 percent of the seats in the stadium were empty. To add to the pain, half the fans in the stands were rooting for the other team. To deal with the problem, Blank went around the city asking people why they were not purchasing tickets to our games. "Why don't you come to the Georgia Dome?" he asked. Blank and his colleagues made a list of the problems and fixed them. He noted that in his first 15 years as owner, 13 of the years were sellouts.

Blank added that if you have the humility to listen to listen to people rather than just hawking merchandise or services, you will have a lot of customers. Too many business people have egos too big to bother to ask.[15]

Another practical approach to developing empathy is to suspend judgment so you can understand the other person's perspective. It is easy to jump to a conclusion instead of carefully considering what the other person is experiencing, thinking, or feeling.[16] Imagine that a manager is discussing a possible promotion with a direct report. The employee is showing some hesitation, and the manager assumes that the employee might want to avoid additional responsibility. With gentle questioning, the manager might find out that the employee is concerned about longer hours and possible travel that would conflict with personal life.

Look for Opportunities to Express Gratitude

Humble leaders and professionals readily express gratitude. You can therefore develop and enhance your humility by seeking out opportunities to express gratitude. A basic starting point is to be grateful for what you have to be thankful for, or as the adage says, "Count your blessings." The next step is more difficult. Look for opportunities to express gratitude in everyday life and in the workplace. Express gratitude to your tireless postal carrier or truck driver for his or her faithful deliveries. Thank the receptionist at the hotel for getting your online reservation straight. In the workplace show gratitude for the caterer who gets the lunch order correct and on time. Then move on toward leadership humility by thanking the team for getting a complicated project completed correctly and on time.

Celebrate the Success of Others

Given that celebrating the success of others is a characteristic behavior of leaders with humility, another effective way of being a humble leader is to make a conscious effort to celebrate the strong accomplishments of group members. Humble leaders acknowledge both individual and team accomplishments and celebrate that success.[17] What constitutes an appropriate celebration depends on both the magnitude of the success and the time and money available for the celebration. Among the possibilities would be a 30-minute refreshment break, a dinner or lunch celebration, an intranet post, or a mention of accomplishment during a meeting.

Celebrating the success of others can also take the modest form of passing along to the team credit for the recognition you receive. A representative statement to the team would be, "It makes me happy to announce that the C-suite folks are thrilled with the new software we developed for taking care of routine inquiries."

Embrace a Spirit of Service

Following the model of the servant leader, an effective way of becoming a humble leader is to be service-oriented. Consult with your group to analyze what you can do to help them succeed. Employees can readily figure out which leaders are committed to helping them to succeed versus those who are hustling for personal success.[18] Responses to the question of "How can I help you succeed?" vary considerably, and the leader has to choose which demands are feasible. Here is a sampling of responses to the question at hand:

- "We need more money for equipment including software."
- "I can't concentrate on my work if I have to attend 8 a.m. virtual meetings and get my two children off to school at the same time."
- "We could do a better job of getting deliverables on time if you made fewer changes in plans of what you wanted us to do."
- "We can't possibly improve customer service if we do not hire two more support technicians. Our workload is a bone crusher."

Give Others Freedom to Perform their Work

Leaders who micromanage are perceived as too controlling to be humble. It therefore follows logically that a robust way of developing humility as a leader is to give group members more freedom to perform their work. The developmental challenge here for the leader who likes to tightly control the work of others and limit their freedom to work independently is that personality traits are a factor. The trait of perfectionism is a key factor. If you have the tendency of perfectionists to have the urge to correct the work activities of others, it will be difficult to grant the freedom to perform their work.

You will have to think carefully about tasks you can grant subordinates freedom to perform, and which tasks must be more tightly controlled. Luke, a vice president of finance, might recognize that it is natural for him to intervene in the work of group members because all their work involves the precious resource of money. Luke therefore has to painfully compose a list of group member tasks that he will involve himself in versus those tasks he will grant more freedom. To illustrate, Luke might think, "I will definitely get closely involved when a group member is working on investing company money in hedge funds. But my only action when a group member is investing in money market funds is to grant final approval."

Understand the Big Picture of the Team

Angela Sebaly, co-founder and CEO of Personify Leadership, observes that humble leaders are focused on the big picture of the team and its mission rather than themselves. "Humility is about minimizing the self and maximizing the bigger purpose you represent," Sebaly said. "When you think about humility in that way, it becomes a vital competency in leadership because it takes the focus from 'I' to 'We.'"[19] The developmental perspective here is to stop and think about the big picture of what the team is attempting to accomplish rather than about personal concerns.

Assume that team leader Gwenn is on an assignment that she thought would only last one year. Her intent was to use the team leader assignment as a stepping stone to a project manager position. Gwenn is informed that she will have to stay with the team for an additional year because its project will be much longer than anticipated. To develop her humility, Gwenn introspects, "To be humble I have to focus on what the team needs to accomplish, not on my own career advancement. After all, I want to be an honorable leader."

Big-picture thinking is such a key part of being humble that you are invited to take the accompanying self-quiz.

MY TENDENCIES TOWARD BIG-PICTURE THINKING

Indicate your strength of agreement with each of the following statements: SD—*Strongly Disagree*; D—*Disagree*; N—*Neutral*, A—*Agree*; SA—*Strongly Agree*.

Statement about Big-Picture Thinking	SD	D	N	A	SA
1. I get upset if my checkbook does not balance even to the dollar.	5	4	3	2	1
2. I often think about the meaning and implication of news stories.	1	2	3	4	5
3. A top-level manager is usually better off finding ways to cut costs than thinking about the future of the business.	5	4	3	2	1
4. I like to argue (or used to) with an instructor about what should be the correct answer to a multiple-choice question.	5	4	3	2	1

Statement about Big-Picture Thinking	SD	D	N	A	SA
5. So long as a company provides good customer service with its present product line, its future is very secure.	5	4	3	2	1
6. I prefer acquiring knowledge and skills that can help me with my job during the next month rather than those that might help me in the future.	5	4	3	2	1
7. It makes me laugh when a CEO says a big part of his or her job is creating visions.	5	4	3	2	1
8. I have already created a vision for my life.	1	2	3	4	5
9. I am a big-picture thinker.	1	2	3	4	5
10. If people take care of today's problems, they do not have to worry about the future.	5	4	3	2	1
11. World events have very little impact on my life.	5	4	3	2	1
12. An organization cannot become great with an exciting vision.	1	2	3	4	5

Scoring and Interpretation: Find your total score by summing the point values for each question.

52–60: You are probably already a big-picture thinker which should help you in your career.

30–51: You probably have a neutral, detached attitude toward thinking big.

12–29: Your thinking probably emphasizes the here and now and the short term. People in this category usually do not focus on the implications of their work.

Observe Models of Humility

A good deal of learning in most professions and trades takes place via modeling the behavior—the classic apprentice and master (or mentor) relationship. Despite the digitalization of a high percentage of life, we still learn many valuable skills by observing others, including how to change a tire or surgically remove a brain tumor. Perhaps you know a leader you consider to be humble, then take the opportunity to observe how he or she interacts with others. An alternative but weaker approach would be to identify a leader acknowledged to be humble, such as Mary Barra of

GM, and then search for any appearance that may have been recorded on YouTube.

When you attempt to model some of the behaviors of a humble leader, look for subtle signs of humility, such as how easily the leader gives credit to others. A telling observation is to look for how frequently the person uses the "I," versus the "we," with "we" being humbler. Frequent use of the second-person pronoun "you" is humbler than the frequent use of "me." More reliance on the third-person (he, she, him, her, and "they") is humbler than heavy reliance on "I," or "me."

CARL WANG: A HUMBLE LEADER WHOSE INVENTION HAS PREVENTED BLINDNESS IN FIVE MILLION PEOPLE

MID Labs (Medical Instrument Development Laboratories, Inc.) of San Leandro, California, was founded by Carl Wang in 1981. The company soon became a global leader in the manufacture of ophthalmic surgical devices. Under the leadership and creativity of Wang, MID Labs pioneered the tools for modern vitrectomy. A vitrectomy is an eye surgery that cuts and removes the gel-like vitreous fluid from the eyeball without damaging the retina. The branded product line of MID Labs is supplied to more than 30 countries globally. The company was acquired by HOYA Surgical Optics in 2019.

One of Carl Wang's early goals was to develop a disposable cutter design which would be affordable in third-world countries. Since its inception, MID Labs has made enough disposable cutters to keep more than 5 million people worldwide from going blind due to injuries and diseases like diabetes. Almost 100 percent of all cutters sold by competitors today are descendants of Wang's original design.

Andrew Wang, the son of Carl Wang, is an electrical engineer who began working at ML (a favored employee abbreviation for MID Labs) in 1992 when there were only five employees. The younger Wang stayed with the company until 2019, and has provided the first-hand facts and insights into the company and its founder that are reported here. His last position with the company was director of project management. He has stayed in touch with many ML employees. Carl Wang passed away in 2011, and the company shifted to a more, formal corporate-like identity.

MID employees are still strongly influenced by Carl Wang's mantra that "We can achieve anything working together." Company employees strongly believe that product quality and helping each other are key values, and the older Wang emphasized that employees were responsible for the company's success.

In 2008, the office manager at MID created a patent wall that listed company patents that were attributed both to Carl Wang and company employees. Yet Wang never talked much about the wall. He perceived the primary value of the patents to help in making alliances and friendships with ophthalmology surgeons. He gave credit to many ophthalmologists for developing new surgical procedures needed to maximize the benefits to the patient.

Carl Wang was a leader with humility in a multitude of ways, such as being on a first-name basis with work associates instead of being called "Dr. Wang." The senior Wang enjoyed having lunch with employees, most frequently with the lowest-paid assembly line employees. These employees were the heart of MID because the tiny and complex surgical tools, with a hollow tube-in-tube and an embedded cutter, are mostly handmade. Quality is dependent on assembler patience and care, and working with each other and with engineers and quality control when problems occur.

The younger Wang explained that his father's humility facilitated creating a company of dedicated and loyal employees who innovated new surgical tools for better patient outcomes. They worked as a team to launch better products and achieve the sharpest cutter in the industry.

The service-to-others aspect of the humility of Wang surfaced when he set out to create a company where people would enjoy working hard as a team, accomplish something meaningful, and make money. He decided to start a company that would help keep people from going blind. As an engineer, Wang was often on the production floor working with assemblers to solve problems. But this problem-solving really started in the lunchroom, where open discussion allowed for trust and camaraderie.

MID employees understood implicitly that their leader took their ideas seriously. An outstanding example is that they independently came up with this mission statement: "To excel at providing quality and innovative ophthalmic products that benefit patients around the world." They had a banner made containing the mission statement and placed it in the conference room. Wang believed so strongly that employees were the backbone of the company's success that he accepted the mission statement with enthusiasm.

Despite the contribution and acceptance of MID's products, the company went through two difficult financial periods. Twice when the company was about to go bankrupt, many employees banded together and worked harder without a paycheck to save the company. Andrew Wang contends the unusual employee effort could be attributed to the workforce believing in the mission of the company, and loyalty to his father. Many employees worked decades, up until retiring.

When Wang was dying of an incurable illness, he told people not to fuss over him. This is the only time employees, surgeons, and friends actively disobeyed. Three hundred people showed up for Wang's memorial. Many people spoke of his genius, but would also emphasize that he was a friend.

Carl Wang supported himself through college as an immigrant working as a waiter in a Chinese restaurant. Wang studied electrical engineering at Taida University in China for two years. After moving to the United States, he received a bachelor's degree and then a PhD in electrical engineering from the University of Illinois Urbana Champaign, graduating near the top of his class.[20]

GUIDELINES FOR ACTION

1. Humility is a trait, behavior, and skill that can be developed with appropriate knowledge on the subject plus the self-discipline to apply the knowledge.
2. If you develop a hunger to learn it helps make you humble because the hunger points to so much knowledge in the outside world that you do not already possess.
3. Admitting that you do not know something is a basic characteristic of a humble person.
4. Being okay with being wrong is a necessary and important part of developing humility.
5. Thinking that there is something in the external world more important than yourself can help develop your humility.
6. If you model what you want others to do, you are both humble and perceived as humble.
7. An easy way to feel humble is to reflect on mistakes and setbacks you have experienced.

8. A key component of humility is to understand your limitations and weaknesses.

9. A key strategy for being a humble leader is to hold yourself accountable for something that goes wrong under your command.

10. To come across as humble make ample use of self-deprecating humor.

11. A subtle way of demonstrating humility is to recognize how you might be contributing to conflict with another person.

12. The most systematic way of developing and enhancing humility is to obtain feedback from a variety of sources. The feedback can be for formal programs or informal comments.

13. An effective way of developing humility is to obtain input from others before making a decision.

14. Finding ways to improve your empathy is a natural way of enhancing your humility. Asking people questions about how they see things is an effective starting point.

15. You can develop and enhance your humility by seeking out opportunities to express gratitude.

16. To have humility as a leader or professional, make a conscious effort to celebrate the strong accomplishments of group members.

17. An effective way of becoming a humble leader is to be service-oriented.

18. A robust way of developing humility as a leader is to give group members more freedom to perform their work.

19. To enhance your humility as a leader to team members focus on the big picture of the team and its mission rather than on yourself.

20. When you attempt to model the behaviors of humble leaders, look for subtle signs of humility, such as how easily the leader gives credit to others.

NOTES

1. Quoted in "Humility is a Key to High Performance and Effective Leadership," www.foster.com.uw.edu, September 19, 2012, p. 3.

2. Toby Cosgrove, "Medical Leadership Calls for Humility, Self-Awareness," *Consult QD* (https://consultqd.clevelandclinic.org), September 18, 2016, p. 1.

3. IW Staff, "Humility: Your No 1 Leadership Asset for 2016," *Industry Week* (www.industryweek.com), January 7, 2016, p. 5.

4. Peter Barron Stark, "9 Habits of Humble Leaders," *Peterstark.com*, July 7, 2016, p. 1.

5. Quoted in IW Staff, "Humility: Your Number 1 Leadership Asset," p. 5.

6. Randy Conley, "Think You're Wise in Your Own Eyes? 4 Steps to Develop Leadership Humility," *Leading with Trust* (www.leadingwithtrust.com), © 2011 The Ken Blanchard Companies, p. 2.

7. Quint Studer, "What Does Humble Leadership Look Like in Action," *Pensacola News Journal* (pnj.com), April 27, 2019, p. 1.

8. Russ S. Moxley, "Hardships," In Cynthia D. McCauley, Russ D. Moxley, and Ellen Van Velsor, Editors, *The Center for Creative Leadership Handbook of Leadership Development* (San Francisco: Jossey-Bass Publishers, 1998), p. 199.

9. Bill Treasurer, "Why Successful Leaders Need to Learn Humility," *Success* (www.success.com), December 16, 2016, p. 2.

10. McPhee Andrewartha, "Leadership Tip # 3: Humility is a Leadership Skill," *MCA Group* (www.mcpheeandrewarth.com.au), February 24, 2015, p. 2.

11. Conley, "Think You're Wise in Your Own Eyes?" p. 1.

12. Jess Johnson, "Humility in Leadership: Battling the Vices of Pride," *Crowdstaffing* (www.crowdstaffing.com/blog), May 1, 2018, p. 2.

13. Erik Hoestra, Anthony Bell, and Scott R Peterson, "Humility in Leadership: Abandoning the Pursuit of Unattainable Behavior." In S. A. Quatro & R. R. Sims (Eds.), *Executive Ethics: Ethical Dilemmas and Challenges for the C-Suite* (Greenwich, CT: Information Age Publishing, 2008), p. 22.

14. Sabina Nawaz, "Get the Accountable Feedback You Need to Get Promoted," *Harvard Business Review* (https://hbr.org), October 31, 2017, p. 3.

15. "Humility by Arthur Blank," *Forbes 100th Anniversary Issue*, September 28, 2017, p. 136.

16. IW Staff, "Humility: Your No 1 Leadership Asset for 2016," p. 4.

17. Stark, "9 Habits of Humble Leaders," p. 2.

18. John Dame and Jeffrey Gedmin, "Six Principles for Developing Humility as a Leader," *Harvard Business Review* (https://hbr.org), September 9, 2013, p. 3.

19. Quoted in Karina Fabian, "Humble Leadership: Why Humility Matters for Managers" *Business News Daily* (www.businessnewsdaily.com), March 6, 2017, p. 2.

20. Original story based on facts and observations in a personal communication from Andrew Wang, July 17, 2023; "MiDLABS (Medical Instrument Development Laboratories, Inc." July 29, 2016, pp. 1.

10

Making Effective Use of Humility

All of what has been described in this book so far deals with the application of humility to enhance leadership and professional effectiveness. In this final chapter we highlight actions you can take to make optimum use of humility in your repertoire. To repeat, humility alone will not drive career success but must be integrated into other effective leadership and professional behaviors.

A representative example is Michelle, the head of human resources who thinks of an imaginative way to advance the contribution of her team to the total organization. Michelle proposes to top-level management that her group provide tutoring to help remote workers become more productive when working from home. Suddenly the human resources group is flooded with requests to enhance the productivity of individual remote workers. When asked about how she came up with such a useful idea, Michelle does not refer to her own creative problem-solving skills. Instead, Michelle says, "We have such a fine group of people in our HR department. We regularly bat around ideas, so you could say I was probably piggybacking on the idea of one of our talented professionals."

COMBINE HUMILITY WITH OTHER ATTRIBUTES OF EFFECTIVE LEADERS

As alluded to above, the key theme of this book is that humility combined with other leadership and professional attributes enhances effectiveness. Humility facilitates leadership success when it is combined with other standard attributes of effective leaders. Sprinkle in a little humility, and

DOI: 10.4324/9781003461784-10

other leadership attributes make an even stronger contribution to effectiveness. Research has demonstrated dozens of different attributes linked to leadership effectiveness across many different situations and contexts. Next, we look at how humility can enhance the utility of seven important attributes of successful leaders and professionals.

1. *Drive and Passion.* Leaders are noted for the effort they invest in their work and the passion they have for work and work associates. The drive and passion often expresses itself as an obsession for achieving company goals. Without a little humility, such as recognizing the contribution of others, the leader might appear so work-obsessed that he or she loses out on the total support of some subordinates. It can be uncomfortable working for a work-obsessed person who seems to ignore the contribution of others.

2. *Self-Confidence.* Self-confidence contributes to effective leadership in several ways. Above all, self-confident leaders project an image that encourages subordinates to have faith in them. Self-confidence also helps leaders make some of the tough business decisions they face regularly. When a dose of humility, such as placing other people in the limelight, is combined with self-confidence, the leader is likely to be even more influential.

3. *Proactivity.* Leadership is almost synonymous with taking the initiative and being proactive includes taking the initiative to work on problems. The proactive person makes things happen as part of his or her work role. As a result, a leader with a proactive personality is more likely to be able to influence people and bring about constructive change. Carried to extremes, proactive leaders can be an annoyance because they focus so much on upending the status quo. A little humility can soften the proactivity, such as the leader saying "I am not an expert on how you detail cars for customers, but maybe as an outsider I might see a small area for improvement."

4. *Trustworthiness and Honesty.* Trust is regarded as one of the major leadership attributes. Effective leaders know they must build strong employee trust to obtain high productivity and commitment. Trustworthy leaders practice what they preach and set an example. Humility enhances trustworthiness and honesty because humble people are trusted more than their bombastic counterparts. An effective way of showing humility is by allowing group members

to participate in decision-making. Sharing information with group members is another fundamental trust-builder that is also a sign of humility. A robust example is sharing detailed information about plans for the expansion or construction of the organization or organizational unit.

5. *Good Intellectual Ability, Knowledge, and Technical Competence.* Effective leaders are good problem-solvers and knowledgeable about the business or technology for which they are responsible. They are likely to combine analytical intelligence with practical intelligence (the ability to solve everyday problems based on experience). Intelligence, knowledge, and technical competence are more likely to be influential when the leader or professional adds a touch of humility to the mental prowess.

You have probably observed that some people use their smarts in an aggressive, offensive way that might alienate, rather than win over other people. The leader or professional can appear humbler with statements such as, "Here are a couple of relevant facts I came upon that could give us a little more direction" or "Here is some new evidence that might influence our thinking."

6. *Sense of Humor.* An effective sense of humor is an important part of a leader's job. In the workplace, humor relieves tension and boredom, defuses hostility, and helps build relationships with group members. The leader or professional who makes the occasional witty comment is likely to be perceived as approachable and friendly. Humor also builds positive relationships with subordinates, which in turn results in group members being better organizational citizens (being helpful to others).[1]

As we described previously, being self-deprecating adds humility to humor. Equally important, a sense of humility will block a leader from using hostile humor. Such humor lessens a leader's effectiveness because it alienates group members. Hostile workplace humor includes assigning unflattering nicknames to work associates and poking fun at people in an insulting manner. An example of the former is referring to an IT-savvy person as "Digit Head." An example of the latter is asking a financial analyst if he graduated last in his class in high school.

7. *Emotional Intelligence.* Emotional intelligence has come to mean almost any human attribute but cognitive ability. More precisely,

emotional intelligence refers to the ability to do such things as understand one's feelings, have empathy for others, and regulate one's emotions to enhance one's quality of life. The ability to minimize temper tantrums is also part of emotional intelligence. A person with high emotional intelligence would therefore ordinarily understand the importance of humility and would be appropriately humble. Unlike the six illustrative leadership traits already described, humility might be considered part of this type of intelligence. Nevertheless, if you remember to emphasize the humility aspects of emotional intelligence—such as empathy—your emotional intelligence with be enhanced and strengthened.

Richard Anderson, the former chief executive of Delta Airlines, provides us with an everyday example of the relevance of the humility aspects of emotional intelligence. He says that the most important leadership lesson he has learned is to be patient and not lose his temper. Anderson notes that when a leader loses his or her temper it squelches debate and sends the signal about how you want your organization to run.[2] (Losing your temper and squelching debate are unhumble actions.)

BE HUMBLE WITH ALL STAKEHOLDERS

Many leaders are accused of being two-faced because they are polite and cordial toward superiors and perhaps customers and coworkers, but rude and inconsiderate toward subordinates. Similarly, humility is sometimes practiced in a two-faced manner which makes the inconsistently humble leader appear inauthentic. It is more effective to be humble toward all stakeholders, thereby enhancing authenticity and effectiveness.

Tara Comonte, the former president of Shake Shack, whose story was reported earlier in this book, is a positive example of being humble with all stakeholders. She is polite, cordial, and a little self-effacing when dealing with the management team and with frontline workers at the restaurants she visits. Part of her across-the-board humility of a commitment to diversity and inclusion, empowerment, and accountability. Comonte has a reputation for sharing blame, or blaming herself, when something goes wrong at Shake Shack.

INCORPORATE A SHARED VISION INTO YOUR LEADERSHIP

Some leaders invest a lot of their time into creating visions, including Kim Jordan of the Belgium Brewery, as described at the end of this chapter. Yet some of these visionaries neglect the reality that a vision must be shared with others, and requires many people to implement. Some management writers even argue that a vision should incorporate the input of many stakeholders. As said by brand-building specialist, Kathy Heasley, "Leadership is being bold enough to have vision and humble enough to recognize achieving it will take the efforts of many."[3]

In addition to receiving input about vision formation, a key component of displaying humility with respect to visioning is to periodically discuss the vision with constituents. A vision is supposed to inspire employees to work toward attaining the vision, which makes obtaining employee reactions to the vision useful. Suppose the CEO develops the generic vision of "To make the world a better place." Almost any company would like to make the world a better place from a tattoo parlor to a manufacturer of space rockets. The CEO might modestly ask company managers and employees how well the vision is working in terms of daily inspiration. Because the CEO is humble and open to suggestions, the comments suggesting a need for refinement of the vision might include:

"Quite frankly, I get more inspiration from the back of the cereal boxes on my kitchen table."
"What are we supposed to do to make the world a better place?"
"Could we form a committee to help tweak this vision to make it more specific?"

To make effective use of humility the CEO could return to the drawing board to refine the vision. The employees with negative comments about the vision might be invited to work on improving the vision.

LEAD BY ACTIONS RATHER THAN BY WORDS

Leading by actions rather than words might be considered a variation of leading by example. Finding ways to demonstrate that you are willing to do what you want others to do helps you make effective use of humility. The same approach might be regarded as converting your values into action. Assume that Crystal is a division president at a consumer products company. She announces during a town hall meeting that the division should be an important contributor to the welfare of the community. In a humble fashion, Crystal asks the employees to nominate by email the two charities in the community they think are the worthiest. She says she will then donate 5 percent of her current salary to the two charities receiving the most votes.

It could be that many division employees will follow the model of Crystal in donating to private charities. Even if the total donations to local charities are not enormous, Crystal will have demonstrated a key behavior of a humble leader—putting her values into action.

SHARE THE POWER OF YOUR POSITION

Power sharing is characteristic of humble leaders, pointing to the logical conclusion that sharing the power of your position will make effective use of your humility. As career coach Christopher Walls observes, by enabling team members to make decisions, you demonstrate confidence in them and build a stronger, more productive and satisfied team. If team members are required to have you review every detail by you before taking action neither you nor your team will reach full potential.[4]

As with any suggestion for making effective use of humility, judgment is required as to which types of decisions and types of power should be shared. Perhaps your organizational unit has been given a choice of which meeting technology to choose among several options. Here would be a good opportunity for you to make effective use of humility by arriving at a group consensus about whether to choose Zoom, Go to Meeting, or Google Meeting, assuming these are the three choices. In contrast, you might have been given direct evidence from the corporate security department that a group member has been selling trade secrets to a competitor. If you decide to recommend that the group member in question should be fired, you should not share this incident of decision-making power with the group.

ASK LOADS OF QUESTIONS

An easy way to make effective use of humility is to ask loads of questions because such actions indicate that you do not think you have all the answers. Instead, you want to capitalize on the knowledge, talent and imagination of others. As an executive coaching newsletter explains, "Humble people know that asking questions doesn't make you weak or stupid. If anything, asking questions makes you a stronger person both mentally and physically."[5]

The most useful questions for making effective use of humility indicate a genuine interest on the part of the questioner in gathering the other person's opinion. Responding with enthusiasm to the response enhances the genuineness of the question. As is often stated, asking an open-ended question is best for gathering rich data from the respondent. Here are two examples of the difference between a close-ended and an open-ended question:

Close-ended: "Do you like my plan for boosting revenue?"
Open-ended: "What are your thoughts about my plan for boosting revenue?"
Close-ended: "Are you satisfied with my vision for our company?"
Open-ended: "In what way do you think my vision for the company could be improved?"

ASK FOR HELP

Asking for help is similar to asking loads of questions. The humble leader or professional demonstrates that by asking for help he or she cannot effectively carry out the leadership role working alone—outside assistance is needed. David Feely from the Institute for Healthcare Improvement notes that asking for help with difficult problems gets surprising results.[6] It is also a robust way of making effective use of humility.

EMBRACE AMBIGUITY AND UNCERTAINTY

Ambiguity and uncertainty pervade today's business environment which provides a good opportunity to make effective use of humility. As noted by business consultant Denyse Whillier, when leaders have the humility to admit that they do not have all the answers, they create space for group members to set forward and propose solutions to vexing problems. The display of humility increases the likelihood that they will receive the valid information they need for good decision-making.[7]

Brandon, an executive in the headquarters of a chain of fast-food restaurant, is convinced that a business recession is fast approaching. The uncertainty he faces, however, is what will be the implications for franchise operators and company-owned stores (restaurants). Will a recession trigger a spurt in demand at the stores because many consumers will shun both expensive and moderately priced restaurants, and flock to fast-food outlets? Or will the recession be so deep that many consumers will even cut back on fast-food dining? The answers to these questions will influence the advice headquarters gives to store managers about staffing for the short term.

Here is a good opportunity for Brandon to make effective use of humility by consulting with his executive team about what advice they should dispense to the store managers. Brandon says to the team, "We have a big decision to make. I don't have a solution to the problem, and I need your input."

ACT LIKE A MEMBER OF THE GROUP WHEN APPROPRIATE

Depending on your need for having high status, another effective way of using humility is to act like a group member. If you have a strong need to create psychological space between you and the group members, this approach would be uncomfortable. According to Christopher Walls, when team members consider the leader to be another member of the team, they will often feel inspired to follow and trust their leader. If the leader appears to be a member of the group, he or she will be seen as approachable and fully engaged with them, the leader will foster a culture of collaboration and create bonds of loyalty that facilitate team success.

In contrast, a leader who unhumbly takes frequent opportunities to remind others of his or her exalted position will be seen as more concerned about personal welfare than advancing the team. By frequently pulling rank, the leader risks becoming isolated and out of touch with the team which hampers collaboration.[8] (This approach to leadership overlooks the contribution of humility to leadership effectiveness.)

ROLL WITH YOUR MISTAKES

When you make a mistake on the job as a leader or corporate professional, here is a good opportunity to make effective use of humility. A mistake can be translated into a valuable moment of leadership. To help turn your gaffe into gold, be transparent, candid and own up to the error, and do not try to blame others. Issue an apology if necessary. All of these actions will enhance the effectiveness of your humility. Yet you could weaken your leadership if you over-apologize or continue to agonize over the mistake.

Strategic management specialist Paul Schoemaker says that the best kinds of mistakes are where the costs are low but the learning is high. If the error was the result of a poor decision, display your humility by explaining to your boss and other interested parties how you will avoid making the same or similar mistake in the future. By demonstrating that you have learned as a result of your mistake, you reassure stakeholders that you can be trusted with equally important assignments or decisions in the future.[9]

An example of making effective use of humility took place at a nonprofit agency that provides child adoption services. The CEO was primarily responsible for hiring a developmental officer (fundraiser) for the agency. Within the first two months on the job, the new developmental officer was accused of multiple actions of blatant sexual harassment and sexual aggression against staff members. After an investigation substantiated many of these acts of sexual harassment, the developmental officer was dismissed.

The CEO apologized to other staff members, and admitted that the developmental officer was not vetted carefully enough. He also explained how the agency would minimize the chances of this type of selection error taking place again. By admitting his mistake humbly, most staffers did not direct blame toward the CEO for having hired a sexual predator.

━━━━━━━━━━━━━

SELECT HUMBLE LEADERS

A natural way for organizations to make effective use of humility is to select leaders and professionals who possess an optimum degree of humility. *Selection* here includes hiring candidates from the outside, as well as promotions from within. A four-trait framework has been developed to evaluate candidates for leadership positions that focus on humility and do not place too much emphasis on charisma and ambition. The four key traits are as follows:

- *Curiosity.* Defined as being driven to proactively seek understanding and new learning. Learning through feedback is included in the curiosity trait.
- *Insight.* People with insight process information from many sources and use it to develop insights that make sense of ambiguity and depart from the status quo.
- *Engagement.* Defined as the ability to engage the hearts and minds of others to deliver shared objectives and mutual benefits. A person with a high standing on engagement, gains energy from authentically connecting with others and understanding them on a deep level.
- *Determination.* People with determination enjoy a challenge but avoid letting their strength of purpose become stubbornness and rigidity. This type of person will assume risks with ingenuity and tenacity, but can nimbly change direction as needed.[10]

There are three major approaches to selecting humble leaders and professionals, all focusing on these and other relevant traits and behaviors. One approach is for the management team to use individual or panel interviews to look for humble characteristics in the external or internal candidate. A second approach is to speak carefully to people who have worked with the candidate about his or her humility. This is the vetting process. A third approach is to use the services of an industrial and organizational psychologist to help with the assessment. The psychologist is likely to use an interview, personality testing, and perhaps give the candidate a simulated job task and look for signs of humility.

A checklist follows that could prove useful in screening for humility when interviewing the candidate. Several of the points raised in the checklist might also be asked of other people about the candidate who have worked with the person.

CHECKLIST FOR MAKING INTERVIEW OBSERVATIONS ABOUT CANDIDATE'S HUMILITY

1. Does the candidate make reference to "I" and "me" and almost never mention the contributions of others?
2. Does the candidate appear to exaggerate his or her accomplishments?
3. Does the candidate ask the interviewer any questions about him or her or the company?
4. Does the candidate appear bored when the interviewer makes any comments about himself or herself?
5. Does the candidate make any reference to the contributions of his or her team members?
6. Does the candidate read or send text messages during the interview?
7. Does the candidate show any appreciation for the opportunity to be interviewed for this position?
8. Is the candidate able to describe any personal weaknesses or setbacks?
9. When asked, is the candidate able to describe any situation in which the group enabled him or her to solve a problem?
10. By the end of the interview did you feel a little sick of hearing how wonderful the candidate is?

Consultants Karl Alleman and Julie Kalt present a case history of the successful hiring of an executive based heavily on the candidate's humility. A division head of a global economy was promoted to become CEO, and a replacement was needed. The chief human resources officer (CHRO) hired outside consultants Alleman and Kalt to conduct an assessment of the three contenders. The CHRO wanted an objective assessment because company leadership and the board thought there was a clear front-runner. He was currently head of the company's largest division, and was self-confident and charismatic. The second contender had a good reputation for being analytical and reliable. Contender number three was the least well known, and was introverted and less flashy than the other two candidates.

The assessment by the consultants revealed that the least obvious contender was a stronger leader than the other two. He was much more effective in developing people and bringing about commitment from the team. He was interested in the new position but expressed his interest in a low-key manner. The presumed best candidate had a more top-down leadership style and was a poor listener which led to challenges in collaborating with and developing his staff. The board agreed with the consultants and decided to choose the least obvious candidate, and he successfully grew the division. The consultants concluded that the third candidate's humility enhanced his success as a division head.[11]

A LEADER WHO BLENDS HUMILITY WITH OTHER KEY ATTRIBUTES: KIM JORDAN, EXECUTIVE CHAIR OF NEW BELGIUM BREWING

Kim Jordan is the co-founder, and Executive Chair of the Board of Directors of New Belgium Brewing Company, the fourth-largest craft brewer in the United States. Jordan was previously the CEO for six years. New Belgium is now owned by the Kirnin Company, an international beverage conglomerate. Fat Tire is New Belgium's flagship beer. Jordan's present responsibilities focus on developing business strategy and creating visions. She has been ranked as one of the most successful women entrepreneurs in the United States.

Jordan attributes much of the success of the company to a loyal group of employees, most of whom have an ownership stake in the company. Jordan believes that New Belgium has a high-involvement culture of engaged, enthusiastic workers. High morale is indicated by an employee turnover rate of less than 5 percent. In the classic tradition of having humble leadership, employees contribute many ideas about improving company operations as well as the many brands of beer.

At one point, Jordan sold New Belgium to her employees, using an employee stock ownership plan (ESOP). She regarded financially empowering her employees as the right thing to do, and the best move for her business. "I wanted them to have access to some wealth. When I bring it down to a personal level, there's only so much money that I need."

She emphasizes that New Belgium has a high-involvement culture. All workers know where the money goes, and everyone is expected to participate and contribute to strategy development. Jordan believes that she has created a work environment with transparency that has fostered trust and a feeling of togetherness. She believes in transparency as a way of involving employees. All New Belgium employees can access the company intranet and review the company financials to see how corporate money is spent. Sales and performance figures are also reviewed at monthly meetings with employees.

Much of Jordan's early work at New Belgium focused on business strategy as she launched new brews and entered new markets. Early on she established consensus decision-making as a business practice, which gave every employee a voice. It did not mean watering down decisions so everybody loved them. What it did mean is that company leadership talked about the decision enough so that everybody understood the idea enough that they were willing to give their support.

Jordan believes that her best strength is speaking in a straightforward and human way. She also believes that her intuition has contributed heavily to her business success. Yet Jordan also believes that failure contributes to success because we learn from our setbacks.

Jordan relishes seeing other people succeed. Her big audacious goal is to create a national and international amalgamation of craft brewers who can develop and reap the benefits of their entrepreneurial efforts. "I think of it as brewing with friends," she said.

Jordan began her career in social work, which has influenced her humanistic and humble approach to leadership. She emphasizes protecting the external environment and philanthropic giving. Jordan has spoken to thousands of people in business, the nonprofit sector, and academia about how to create a vibrant and rewarding organizational culture that enhances profits and as well as the lives of coworkers and customers.

A brewing industry analyst wrote that Jordan is a classical entrepreneurial success story. She and her former husband had an idea that started as a passion project in a basement, and grew into one of the most successful businesses in its industry. Furthermore, "Jordan has again and again ignored conventional wisdom to create one of the most equitable, sustainable, and community-focused companies around."[12]

In short, Kim Jordan is a creative, strategic thinker with great business acumen who has led her enterprise with humility.

GUIDELINES FOR ACTION

1. If you sprinkle in a little humility, other leadership attributes will make an even stronger contribution to your effectiveness.
2. If you recognize the contribution of others, drive and passion will appear less like a work obsession.
3. A little humility can soften proactivity so you might not be an annoyance to others.
4. An effective way of showing humility is to allow for participative decision-making.
5. Your intelligence, knowledge, and technical competence are more likely to be influential when you add a touch of humility to your mental prowess.
6. If you remember to emphasize the humility aspects of emotional intelligence—such as empathy—your emotional intelligence will be enhanced and strengthened.
7. If you are humble toward all stakeholders, your authenticity and effectiveness will be enhanced.
8. Finding ways to demonstrate that you are willing to do what you want others to do helps you make effective use of humility.
9. Sharing power with group members will help you make effective use of your humility.
10. An easy way to make effective use of humility is to ask loads of questions because such actions indicate that you do not think you have all the answers.
11. Asking for help with difficult and or ambiguous problems is a robust way of making effective use of humility.
12. Depending on your need to be a little distant from the group, an effective way of using humility is to act like a group member.
13. Making a mistake provides a good opportunity to make effective use of humility. Be transparent, candid and own up to the error, and do not blame others.

14. A natural way for organizations to make effective use of humility is to select leaders and professionals who possess an optimum degree of humility.
15. Best of luck in blending humility with your other positive leadership and professional attributes!

NOTES

1. Cecily D. Cooper, Dejun Tony Kung, and Craig D Crossley, "Leader Humor as an Interpersonal Resource Integrating Three Theoretical Perspectives," *Academy of Management Perspectives*, April 2018, pp. 769–796.
2. Cited in Adam Bryant, "He wants Subjects, Verbs, and Objects," *The New York Times* (www.nytimes.com), April 26, 2009, p. 1.
3. Quoted "Humble Leaders," www.discprofiles.com, October 4, 2018, p. 2.
4. Christopher Walls, "Why Humility Is a Key Leadership Trait," www.wallscareer coach.com, December 2018, pp. 1–2.
5. Westfield World Trade Center, "The Importance of Humility," *Gloveworx* (www .gloveworx.com), May 26, 2019, p. 2.
6. Derek Feely, "Health Care Leaders: Heroism Is Out, Humility Is In," *Institute for Healthcare Improvement* (www.ihi.org), March 29, 2018, p. 1.
7. Denyse Whillier, "Humility: An Overlooked Leadership Trait," www.denyse whillier.com, July 4, 2016, p. 4.
8. Walls, "Why Humility Is a Key Leadership Trait," p. 1.
9. Cited in Amy Gallo, "You've Made a Mistake Now What?" http://blogs.hbr.org, April 28, 2010, pp. 1–3.
10. Karl Alleman and Julie Kalt, "We Need More Humble Leaders Here's How to Get Them," *Fast Company* (www.fastcompany.com), June 3, 2019, pp. 1–8.
11. The case history is also from Alleman and Kalt, "We Need More Humble Leaders," pp. 4–5.
12. Original story based on facts and observations in the following sources: "Kim Jordan: Co-Founder, New Belgium Brewing Co." www.californiacraftbeer.com, 2023, pp. 1–3; Keith Gribbins, "Watch Kim Jordan Chronicle the History of New Belgium Brewing," *Craft Brewing Business* (www.craftbrewingbusiness.com), October 7, 2021, p. 1; Kelly K Spors, "What I Love—*and Hate*—Most about Being an Entrepreneur: Kim Jordan," *The Wall Street Journal*, May 11, 2020, p. R2; Jess Baker, "New Belgium Brewing's Kim Jordan Honored Among 2018's 'World-Changing Women,'" Craftbeer.com, January 18, 2018, pp. 1–2.

Index

Printed in the United States
by Baker & Taylor Publisher Services